The Buzz About *Boomer Brands*

When was the last time you had your memory tickled over a long-forgotten but prized product that shaped your childhood? You'll find a lot of those "Oh, yeah, I remember" moments in Barry Silverstein's wonderful wander down Memory Lane. "Try it, you'll like it."
- Ron Schon, Retired Advertising Agency Executive and OLLI Instructor, "The History of Advertising"

Boomer Brands is a delightful book filled with fun facts about our favorite childhood brands and memories. If you're over 50, you're sure to enjoy this nostalgic, entertaining and informative stroll down Memory Lane.
- Nancy Collamer, Career/Retirement Coach and Author, *Second-Act Careers*

If you remember watching Saturday morning TV while slurping down a bowl of Frosted Flakes, or perhaps begged your parents to visit Disneyland after watching Wonderful World of Disney on Sunday night, you'll want to read *Boomer Brands*. This enjoyable, easy read is chock full of fun facts about what made the brands we grew up with iconic.
- Anne Holmes, "Boomer in Chief," National Association of Baby Boomer Women

Barry Silverstein offers a fun walk down Memory Lane for boomers, describing what made some of their favorite childhood brands so treasured then and now.
- Richard Eisenberg, Managing Editor, *Nextavenue.org*

For a delightful look at the products and mores that shaped the lives of the boomer generation, you can't do much better than *Boomer Brands* by Barry Silverstein.
- From a 5-star review by Keith Julius, *ReadersFavorite.com*

Boomer Brands

Iconic Brands that
Shaped Our Childhood

Barry Silverstein

GuideWords Publishing

GuideWords Publishing
5 Blue Damsel Court
Biltmore Lake, NC 28715 USA
www.guidewordspub.com

Cover Design by Charala
Cover illustration licensed under Creative Commons CCO 1.0 Universal Public Domain Dedication
Book Layout © 2017 BookDesignTemplates.com

Boomer Brands – Barry Silverstein -- 1st ed.
Library of Congress Control Number 2018911219
Paperbound ISBN 978-0-9965760-3-1
EPUB edition ISBN 978-0-9965760-4-8
Kindle edition ISBN 978-0-9965760-5-5

Printed in the United States of America

Contents

Boomer Brands
and You

First, a word from our sponsor...

Not a real sponsor, but a fictional one called "Brand."

"Brand" is a much-used, often-maligned marketing term that is revered by product companies and their agencies but, at times, reviled by consumers overwhelmed with brand choice. To put it into the simplest terms, a brand is any distinct product with a name and a set of attributes that distinguishes it from other products, particularly those that compete in the same category. As brands have matured, so too has the way in which they are marketed. Perhaps the most significant thing for you to comprehend about the brand, as a Boomer consumer, is that it can take on a personality and, just like a person or a favorite pet, a brand can be beloved. Yes, that's right, beloved.

The key to effectively marketing a brand is not so much appealing to the rational mind as it is capturing the emotional heart. While there are always rational reasons to purchase a brand, it is the emotional connection a brand develops with a consumer that makes it irresistible. Think about a brand you really, really like – or even love – and you are likely to *feel* something strongly positive about it.

I'll go out on a limb here and suggest to you that, even after all these years, you *still* feel an emotional connection to certain "Boomer Brands" – brands that tunneled their way into your consciousness when you were a kid. You may not even think about them much anymore, but you still feel something when you hear their names today. Remarkably, many of those brands still exist today, 40, 50, or even 60 years after your childhood memories of them. That's the power of "Brand."

We now return to our regularly scheduled Introduction...

As one of the earlier "Baby Boomers" (I was born in 1948), I grew up, as did most of us, watching television. It was this magic box that brought the world into our living rooms, first in black-and-white and then, more incredibly, in color. I was an avid fan of The Lone Ranger, Rin Tin Tin and Superman in black-and-white. When color TV arrived, I was enchanted by The Wonderful World of Disney. But seeing Superman's vivid attire when that show was eventually broadcast in living color– well, that was pretty special!

While television permanently changed media consumption in our country in the 50s and 60s, it also emerged as a primary gateway for brands to be foisted upon the children of America. As kids, we were unwittingly exposed to all sorts of product pitches, some of them voiced by our favorite television stars. Those pitches that appeared on children's TV shows were intentionally designed to influence our young minds. As just one example of the impact of the product pitch, every time mom took kids like you and me to the grocery store, we were sure to call out the names of our favorite cereals until she gave in and tossed one or more boxes into the shopping cart. In fact, it is likely that many of the packaged products that ended up on our breakfast, lunch, and dinner tables back then first appeared in television commercials.

Television shaped the way brands were marketed during the Boomer era. Behind the scenes, though, television was just an emerging advertising medium. Brand marketing was the real story. Consumer behemoth Procter & Gamble is credited with pioneering "brand management" as early as the 1930s. This notion essentially focuses entire teams of brand specialists on marketing individual products.

In the 50s and 60s, the advertising industry pushed brand management to new heights, creating a raft of well-researched, well-marketed strong brands, many of which remained resilient for decades. Agencies began to target Boomers, because by the mid-60s, nearly half the population of the United States was under the age of 25. Advertising agencies embraced creativity and innovation – and sometimes irreverence and brashness. This was a new generation for brands.

"Boomer Brands" largely influenced what we pressed our parents to purchase, and what we ourselves craved as kids. Later on, of course, other things became more important; after all, as we grew up, we became the generation that eschewed commercialism, turned on, tuned in, dropped out, promoted free love, and marched for civil rights, women's equality, and an end to the war in Vietnam.

Still, those Boomer Brands claim a cherished position in our memory banks. How can we forget the brands we grew up with? Chances are, we can't, and we haven't. That's the reason I decided to write this book.

For most of us, our Boomer childhood was a simpler time of riding Schwinn bikes down our streets, watching The Ed Sullivan Show on CBS Sunday nights together with our families, and imagining Tony the Tiger sitting right next to us as we ate our Kellogg's Frosted Flakes for breakfast. So join with me now as I take a comforting stroll down memory lane for a nostalgic look at some of the iconic brands that shaped our childhood.

How to Savor This Book

Each chapter of this book begins with a story about a product category or area of life during the Boomer childhood years, predominantly the 50s and 60s. These stories are written to give some historical context to the category or area, but they are intended to be anything but boring.

Every story is followed by a section that talks about why we loved the brands in that category or area of life. Included in that section is a related list of some of the relevant Boomer era brands. You'll be amazed at how many brands you remember. Each chapter concludes with "Boomer Brand Cameos," brief accounts of specific brands. Cameos focus on brands that have interesting or unique stories to tell. The final chapter highlights ten brands of the Boomer era with lasting legacies. An appendix lists brands and other fun facts for each of the Boomer birth years (1946 to 1964).

You can read this book from start to finish, or you can read chapters in any order. You decide, based on your particular interests. Chapters are self-contained and the content has been organized to make it easy to browse, move around freely, stop anywhere, and reminisce. Trademarks are valuable intellectual property, so they are always listed in each chapter. The sources indicated at the end of the chapters will provide you with expanded information if you are interested.

How can you get the most out of this book? Sit back, relax, and imagine yourself reliving your childhood. It's as simple as that. Just enjoy it and savor the memories.

I hope you have as much fun reading *Boomer Brands* as I had writing it.

The following trademarks and registered trademarks are the property of their respective holders: CBS, Ed Sullivan, Kellogg's Frosted Flakes, Lone Ranger, Procter & Gamble Rin Tin Tin, Schwinn, Superman, Tony the Tiger, Wonderful World of Disney

Sources

http://adage.com/article/adage-encyclopedia/history-1960s/98702/

https://www.theatlantic.com/business/archive/2011/10/how-brands-were-born-a-brief-history-of-modern-marketing/246012/

https://hbswk.hbs.edu/archive/american-business-1920-2000-how-it-worked-pg-changing-the-face-of-consumer-marketing

View Tube

The most influential medium of the Boomer era was undoubtedly television, so that's where *Boomer Brands* begins. During our childhood, television first appeared. By the 60s, television was the dominant medium in America. Radio was still important, but there were neither video games nor the Internet to compete with America's new audio-visual medium. As a result, Boomer kids were truly the TV generation.

What does this have to do with brands? Pretty much everything. Television was fertile ground for brand marketers to reach more of the American population than any other medium. Channel choices were at first limited to three networks, ABC, CBS, and NBC. That meant a brand marketer could easily saturate the market by advertising exclusively on these networks – quite different from the hundreds of free and paid television channel options available today.

Early on, brand marketers recognized they could not only reach adults with their brand messages, but children as well. Why was advertising directly to children desirable? Because kids were a straight route to adults, who ultimately purchased products on their behalf. Over time, parents grew increasingly uncomfortable with the insidious way brand marketers used television to transform very young children (namely us) into product purchase influencers. But there can be no denying that it worked.

The ideal timeslot to advertise to children was Saturday morning. During the 50s and 60s, Saturday mornings were devoted almost exclusively to children's programming. As you'll see in subsequent sections of this book, television programs aimed at kids were sometimes brazenly designed to be nothing more than vehicles for promoting various brands. Then again, television was "free" because it was supported by advertisers, so who could object? And it sure was nice for busy, tired parents to keep their kids engaged on Saturday mornings just by having them turn on the television.

Product brand advertising aside, the shows broadcast on Saturday mornings were, if not always wholesome, highly entertaining for children. They were also surprisingly diverse. Networks dished up plenty of cartoon shows, of course, but there were also educational shows like Mr. Wizard, participation shows like Howdy Doody, and a host of adventure shows across a number of different genres, including Westerns and science fiction.

Each television show was really a brand unto itself. A Saturday morning television show was just as emotionally impactful to the kids who watched it as the branded products the show advertised.

As television matured, children's programming came under fire. In 1961, newly appointed FCC Chairman Newton Minnow famously called television a "vast wasteland," referring in part to children's television shows. Critics derisively characterized TV as the "boob tube." Nevertheless, Saturday morning shows for kids continued for decades – until the 1990 Children's Television Act effectively changed the nature of children's programming, and advertising to children.

Why We Loved Saturday Mornings

What was as good as opening presents on Christmas morning? (Well almost.) Watching television on Saturday mornings, that's what. There you were, with your bowl of undoubtedly sugary cereal in your lap, just you and maybe your siblings, consuming hours of unadulterated entertainment made for kids. It was heaven on earth.

There was a real emotional connection between us and what we watched. These weren't just shows, they resonated with our young, impressionable minds, allowing us to fantasize. They were aspirational because we felt like we were a part of them. Television shows on Saturday mornings hooked us with humor, pathos, adventure, and a good dose of what today would be regarded as downright corny.

Cartoons may have been mindless, but to us, they were laugh-out-loud funny, with characters who were endearing. The old West held a certain fascination for lots of us: Whether it was Annie Oakley, Hopalong Cassidy or The Lone Ranger, we rode along, imagining ourselves doing good and outsmarting bad guys. We spent considerable time flying up in the air, courtesy of shows like Captain Midnight, Sky King and Superman. We fell in love with puppets from Paul Winchell's Jerry Mahoney to Shari Lewis' Lambchop to Sesame Street's Muppets. We learned valuable lessons through the gentle patience and understanding of Mr. Rogers and Mr. Wizard.

And we belonged. We imagined ourselves part of Howdy Doody's Peanut Gallery. We couldn't wait to get Captain Midnight's decoder ring so we could uncover those special messages during the show. We became card-carrying members of the Rin Tin Tin club. We watched the Mickey Mouse Club while wearing our Mousketeer ears and singing along with the theme song.

We may not have realized it, but every one of those Saturday morning shows was a unique brand. TV shows had their own logos, brand platform, and brand characters. They used brand merchandising to sell us toys, games, and clothes. Television characters made personal appearances. Cereal, soft drink, and snack food brands cleverly wove their products into the shows. (You couldn't get that Captain Midnight decoder ring unless you sent in an Ovaltine proof of purchase.)

Before video games even existed, we had our own novel form of video engagement: television on Saturday mornings.

Some of the popular 50s and 60s Saturday morning television shows are listed here. All of these shows appeared on Saturday mornings, unless otherwise noted. Some shows may have also appeared during weekdays or prime time.

Which ones were *your* favorites?

Cartoons

The Adventures of Batman and Robin * The Alvin Show * The Archie Show * Atom Ant * The Banana Splits * Beany and Cecil * The Beatles * The Bugs Bunny Show * The Bullwinkle Show * Casper the Friendly Ghost * Deputy Dawg * Fantastic Voyage * The Flintstones * George of the Jungle * The Hardy Boys * H. R. Pufnstuf * The Huckleberry Hound Show * The Jetsons * Linus the Lionhearted * Mighty Mouse * Mr. Magoo * The New Adventures of Superman * Popeye the Sailor * The Porky Pig Show * Quick Draw McGraw * The Road Runner Show * Scooby-Doo * Spider-Man * Tom and Jerry * Underdog * The Woody Woodpecker Show * Yogi Bear

Live and Film/Video

The Adventures of Kit Carson * The Adventures of Rin Tin Tin * The Adventures of Robin Hood * The Adventures of Superman * Annie Oakley * The Gene Autry Show * The Big Top * Bozo the Clown (weekdays) * Captain Gallant of the Foreign Legion * Captain Kangaroo (weekdays) * Captain Midnight * Circus Boy * Ding Dong School (weekdays) * Fury * Hopalong Cassidy * Howdy Doody * Kukla, Fran and Ollie * Lassie * The Little Rascals * The Lone Ranger * The Mickey Mouse Club * Mr. Rogers' Neighborhood * The Paul Winchell and Jerry Mahoney Show * The Pinky Lee Show * Romper Room (weekdays) * The Roy Rogers Show * Sergeant Preston of the Yukon * Sesame Street (weekdays) * The Shari Lewis Show * Sky King * Space Patrol * Tales of the Texas Rangers * Watch Mr. Wizard * Winky Dink and You

Wizard's World, NBC, The New Adventures of Superman, The Paul Winchell and Jerry Mahoney Show, The Pinky Lee Show, Popeye the Sailor, The Porky Pig Show, Quick Draw McGraw, Rawhide, The Rifleman, The Road Runner Show, Romper Room, Roy Rogers, The Ruff and Reddy Show, Scooby-Doo, Sergeant Preston of the Yukon, Sesame Street, Shari Lewis, Sky King, Space Patrol, Spider-Man, Tales of the Texas Rangers, Tom and Jerry, Underdog, Wagon Train, Watch Mr. Wizard, Winky Dink and You, The Woody Woodpecker Show, Yogi Bear

Sources

http://www.skooldays.com/blog/saturday-in-the-50s/

https://reelrundown.com/animation/Top-Ten-TV-Cartoon-Characters-of-the-1950s-and-1960s

https://groovyhistory.com/top-tv-cartoon-characters-of-the-1950s-and-1960s

https://www.grunge.com/34402/real-reason-saturday-morning-cartoons-disappeared/

http://www.museum.tv/eotv/childrenand.htm

https://en.wikipedia.org/wiki/Bozo_the_Clown

https://en.wikipedia.org/wiki/The_Huckleberry_Hound_Show

http://hanna-barbera.wikia.com/wiki/Huckleberry_Hound

https://www.blogofoa.com/2018/07/john-stewart-teams-up-with-huckleberry-hound.html

http://www.mrwizardstudios.com/

https://www.smithsonianmag.com/smithsonian-institution/meet-mr-wizard-science-guy-inspired-bill-nye-180956371/

https://en.wikipedia.org/wiki/Don_Herbert

https://en.wikipedia.org/wiki/Watch_Mr._Wizard

https://en.wikipedia.org/wiki/Western_(genre)

http://www.filmsite.org/westernfilms.html

https://www.nypl.org/blog/2012/12/01/tv-westerns-1950s-and-60s

Bozo the Clown

Any product brand would envy the remarkable reach and longevity of Bozo the Clown. The Bozo character originated in 1946 in a unique format: a record plus read-along book. Bozo migrated to television in 1949, played by Pinto Colvig, the same actor who voiced the clown on the record. In 1956, actor/producer Larry Harmon purchased the rights to Bozo the Clown. Harmon developed the franchise idea for a half-hour daily local television show with Bozo performing live in front of children, supplemented with cartoons. Hundreds of Bozos sprung up around the country, as well as in France, Germany, and Japan. Harmon then created "Bozo's Big Top" in 1965 for national syndication. While Harmon himself performed the role of Bozo, numerous others played Bozo the Clown. By the mid-60s, Bozo the Clown merchandising was an operation worth over $150 million worldwide. At least one variation of Bozo the Clown continued to air on television until 2001.

Photo credit: "This photo of me, Roger Bowers, in my character of 'Bozo The Clown' when I had the Bozo Show at WJHL-TV, Johnson City, TN in 1960." Licensed under the Creative Commons Attribution-ShareAlike 4.0 International license.

Huckleberry Hound

Huckleberry Hound

Created by the renowned Hanna-Barbera team, Huckleberry Hound was a mild-mannered animated blue dog character who spoke with a bit of a twang. He was introduced in his own television series, "The Huckleberry Hound Show," in 1958, but the show wasn't Hanna-Barbera's first cartoon series – that was "The Ruff and Reddy Show." Huck found himself in all sorts of situations, facing all sorts of villains, but he always prevailed. Interestingly, he seemed to be something of a time traveler, because he appeared as not just himself but as a Roman gladiator, a Medieval knight, and a rocket scientist. Appearing on Huck's show were various other cartoon characters, most notably, Yogi Bear, who became so popular he eventually had a show of his own. In 1960, "The Huckleberry Hound Show" received an Emmy Award, the first animated program to win television's top honor. As a testament to Huckleberry Hound's lasting brand influence, as recently as 2018 his character was teamed up with super-hero Green Lantern in a comic book special set in the 70s.

Photo credit: Huckleberry Hound playing card, Mark Anderson. Licensed under the Creative Commons Attribution 2.0 Generic license.

Mr. Wizard

From 1951 until 1965, kids got a first-hand introduction to science on the weekly TV show, "Watch Mr. Wizard." Mr. Wizard (Don Herbert) conducted science experiments with the help of a young assistant. Mr. Wizard was always patient and encouraging, but he also had a flair for the dramatic. The inspiration behind Mr. Wizard was Don Herbert himself. He proposed the idea for a science show aimed at children to a television station in Chicago. The show's timing was prescient, since it coincided with America's first exploration of space. "Watch Mr. Wizard" was loved by millions of children and won a Peabody Award. Herbert also produced videos, wrote books and sponsored toys, becoming a one-man powerhouse in promoting his own brand. Herbert created an updated version of the show, calling it "Mr. Wizard's World," which ran on Nickelodeon beginning in 1983, exposing a whole new generation of kids to Mr. Wizard.

Photo credit: Publicity photo of Don Herbert from the *Watch Mr. Wizard* television program, NBC Television

Westerns

Westerns have a long and celebrated history in America; in that sense, they represent an enduring brand family. Stories about the emergence of the American West in books and pulp magazines intrigued adults and children alike as early as the 1800s. Westerns naturally made the transition to film, where they enjoyed significant popularity from the 1930s through the 1960s, emerging once again in the 1990s. The Western soon became a staple of American television, both on Saturday mornings and during prime time in the Boomer era. "Hopalong Cassidy" is credited with bringing the Western to TV in 1949. Cassidy was a fictional character from the early 1900s who wore all black (even though he was a good guy). Cassidy was played in more than sixty movies by actor William Boyd. Boyd shrewdly bought the rights to the films, shortened them into television segments, and when they became popular, filmed additional segments as original television shows. Hopalong Cassidy was the first Western TV mega-star, with millions of dollars in brand merchandising, everything from cowboy outfits to lunchboxes to roller skates with spurs. "Hopalong Cassidy" opened the floodgates for other Saturday morning old-time and more contemporary Westerns including "Annie Oakley," "The Gene Autrey Show," "The Lone Ranger," and "The Roy Rogers Show" – and prime time shows like "Bonanza," "Gunsmoke," "Rawhide," "The Rifleman," and "Wagon Train." These shows are still revered by Boomers, who can watch reruns on DVDs, select TV channels and streaming services. Maybe you've even purchased a lunchbox or two at flea markets.

Photo credit: Publicity photo of Clayton Moore as the Lone Ranger and Silver from a personal appearance booking at Pleasure Island (Massachusetts amusement park), Wakefield, Massachusetts, July 30, 1965

Bowled Over

Breakfast cereals are widely regarded as a 20th Century food, but cereal was invented long before it became "The Breakfast of Champions," as the renowned advertising slogan for Wheaties claimed.

The first *hot* ground oatmeal cereal was created as early as 1854 by Ferdinand Schumacher, a German immigrant from Ohio, and the first *cold* breakfast cereal, "Granula" (which had to be soaked overnight for it to be palatable), was the invention of New Yorker James Caleb Jackson in 1863.

So how did cereal brands come to bowl us over during the Boomer era and represent the very heart and soul of the Baby Boomer generation? You can pin that on the brothers Kellogg of Battle Creek, Michigan. (Battle Creek, by the way, is officially known as "the birthplace of cereal." Today, you can pay homage to this beloved breakfast food by attending the annual "National Cereal Festival" there.) John Harvey Kellogg, a surgeon who also ran a health spa in Battle Creek, came up with his own cereal, borrowing the "Granula" name and changing it to "granola" after a legal battle. He then teamed up with brother William and together, they invented Kellogg's Corn Flakes.

William Kellogg, not John, saw the marketing potential of cereal and wanted to build a business around it. You might say he boxed out his brother, buying John's share of their cereal patents. William went on to form the Kellogg Company in 1906. Less than three years later, Kellogg was selling more than a million cases of cereal annually.

Around the same time, a former patient of John Kellogg's health spa named Charles William Post got wind of this cereal thing. He created a cereal called Grape-Nuts, followed by the weirdly named Elijah's Manna, later rechristened Post Toasties (a Kellogg's Corn Flakes knock-off). Guess what? These two products launched the Postum Cereal Company, better known as Post Cereals, a cereal manufacturer that also made its home in Battle Creek.

Fueled by the growing popularity of the new-fangled breakfast cereals, which were originally thought to be healthier than the more traditional egg and meat breakfast of the day, other manufacturers joined the fray.

In the first four decades of the 1900s, the Quaker Oats Company created Puffed Rice and Puffed Wheat, the Washburn Crosby Company (which later became General Mills) produced Wheaties, the Ralston Purina Company came out with Shredded Ralston (the forerunner of the Chex brand), and General Mills introduced Cheerios, originally known as "CheeriOats."

All along, Kellogg was expanding its cereal line, adding such brands as Kellogg's Rice Krispies.

Cereal would become permanently embedded in our lives as the leading American breakfast food.

Why We Loved Cereals

You might say everything changed in the cereal world with the addition of one essential ingredient: Sugar. Oh, and there was another key "ingredient"... you and me, the Baby Boomer kids, who craved sugar.

In 1952, when the first Boomer was around six years old, Kellogg's Sugar Frosted Flakes hit the grocery store shelves. This cereal was really nothing more than the company's flagship Kellogg's Corn Flakes brand with a sugary sheen. That sweet little product introduction dovetailed very nicely with the advent of television. (Eventually, of course, TV was accused of being as bad for the Boomer brain as sugary cereals were for the teeth.)

Television networks quickly recognized that a demographic earthquake was occurring in our country, so they rushed to create programs for families with children. TV followed the model of radio: The programming was free because it was supported by advertising. Millions of little Boomers became a very attractive target audience for children's programs – and what better product to pitch to kids than breakfast cereals?

A lot of children's television programming took advantage of the affection kids had for comic books and cartoons. It was a natural fit for cereal manufacturers, who shamelessly promoted their brands directly to us kids. The manufacturers advertised primarily on children's television shows and often employed animated mascots and cartoon character tie-ins. TV and cereal went together like, well, cereal and milk.

From the very start, cereal manufacturers were brilliant at branding and packaging, reaching their zenith during the Boomer era. Not only did they come up with catchy brand names, cartoon mascots, colorful boxes, and promotional gimmicks – they even gave us unlimited choices by producing those cute little single-serving packages. (Mom or Dad had to cut the thing open, but remember the thrill of pouring milk right into the box?) No wonder cereal brands still occupy the most shelf space of any class of products in modern day grocery stores.

Let's face it. We loved cereal. We *still* love cereal. Some of the popular Boomer era cereal brands are listed below. Which ones were *your* favorites?

General Mills
Cheerios * Cocoa Puffs * Lucky Charms * Kix * Trix * Wheaties
Kellogg
Cocoa Krispies * Frosted Flakes * Froot Loops * Sugar Pops
Maltex
Maypo
Post
Alpha-Bits * Post Toasties * Rice Krinkles
Ralston Purina
Chex
Quaker Oats
Cap'n Crunch * Life

The following trademarks and registered trademarks are the property of their respective holders: Alpha-Bits, American Bandstand, Cap'n Crunch,

Cheerios, Chex, Cocoa Krispies, Cocoa Puffs, Corn Flakes, Disney, Froot Loops, General Mills, Grape-Nuts, Kellogg's, Kellogg's Frosted Flakes, Kellogg's Rice Krispies, Kix, Life, Lone Ranger, Lucky Charms, Maypo, Mickey Mouse Club, Post Cereals, Post Toasties, Puffed Rice, Puffed Wheat, Quaker Oats, Ralston Purina, Rice Krinkles, Rocky and Bullwinkle, Sugar Pops, The Breakfast of Champions, Tony the Tiger, Trix, Wheaties

Sources

https://www.mrbreakfast.com/article.asp?articleid=13

https://www.nytimes.com/interactive/2016/02/22/dining/history-of-cereal.html

http://www.historyofcereals.com/cereal-history/breakfast-cereals/

https://www.seriouseats.com/2015/03/history-of-breakfast-cereal-mascots.html

https://www.delish.com/food-news/g3403/cereal-brands-history/?slide=1

https://www.theatlantic.com/business/archive/2016/06/how-marketers-invented-the-modern-version-of-breakfast/487130/

http://mentalfloss.com/article/74142/8-things-you-might-not-know-about-cheerios

https://www.postconsumerbrands.com/alpha-bits/our-story/

 **Frosted Flakes**

The Kellogg Company was churning out cereals for decades before Boomers came to be. Kellogg's Rice Krispies, for example, was introduced in 1928 with the help of three cartoon pixies named Snap!, Crackle! and Pop! But it was Kellogg's Sugar Frosted Flakes, launched in 1952, that is the generally accepted forerunner of the sugary cereal brands that Boomers came to adore. The Frosted Flakes brand was created for kids, as a sweet variant of the adult version, Kellogg's Corn Flakes. "Tony the Tiger," a cartoon character and "spokescat" for the brand, came to life as an animated barker on television, proclaiming, "They're *Grea-a-a-a-t!*" The company dropped "Sugar" from the name in the 1980s when sugar became widely reviled, but that didn't prevent consumers from continuing to buy the product. Today, Kellogg's Frosted Flakes remains a leading cereal brand, and an updated, more suave version of Tony is still seen on the brand's cereal box.

Cheerios

Originally called CheeriOats when it was introduced by General Mills in 1941, the brand name of this classic cereal was changed to the catchier Cheerios. An unsweetened cereal, comprised of little puffed oat "o's," Cheerios found traction with Boomers largely thanks to television commercials of the 50s featuring the animated "Cheerios Kid," who accomplished heroic tasks after eating Cheerios. In the 60s, print and television advertising for Cheerios regularly employed cartoon characters, such as Rocky and Bullwinkle. Cheerios was also an early innovator in co-branding; for example, Cheerios boxes featured Disney's Mickey Mouse Club, and little toy replicas of the Lone Ranger were packaged inside Cheerios boxes. Cheerios also became one of only two sponsors of Dick Clark's "American Bandstand." It wasn't until the 1970s that the original Cheerios brand was extended to include flavor variations. With the many varieties now found on grocery store shelves, it is no surprise that the Cheerios family is today the best-selling cereal brand.

Photo credit: Tedeytan on VisualHunt.com. Licensed under the Creative Commons Attribution 2.0 Generic license.

 Alpha-Bits

Invented in 1958 by Post Cereals, the Alpha-Bits brand was not only sweet, it was smart: The oat and corn cereal pieces were actual letters of the alphabet. This attribute made it acceptable for kids to play with their cereal – they could actually spell out words in their bowls. In order to compete more effectively in the market, Alpha-Bits became heavily invested in cartoon characters beginning in 1964. The first mascot, "Loveable Truly," was a postman whose mailbag spilled out the Alpha-Bits letters. Loveable Truly was one of several Post cereal characters appearing in "Linus the Lionhearted," a 60s children's cartoon show. Subsequent cartoon mascots included the Alpha-Bits Wizard, Alfie the Alpha-Bits Cereal Wonder Dog, and Alpha the computer. In 1973, Alpha-Bits managed to secure the up-and-coming musical group, The Jackson Five, who recorded "ABC," to appear in television commercials.

Photo credit: Rum Bucolic Ape on Flickr.com. Licensed under the Creative Commons Attribution-NoDerivs 2.0 Generic license.

Life

The Quaker Oats Company, known for its hot oatmeal, entered the cold cereal market in 1961 with the Life brand. This lightly sweetened oat cereal, with a unique rectangular woven pattern, promoted its protein content in direct contrast to most other sugary Boomer era cereals. Instead of relying on cartoon characters, Life launched a television commercial in 1972 that featured a hard-to-please boy named Mikey. When Mikey tries Life, his brothers proclaim with amazement, "Mikey likes it!" Obviously, the commercial was designed to overcome objections by kids to a cereal that highlighted neither sugar nor cartoon mascots. Consumers liked Mikey: The ad campaign became one of the longest running in history (1972 through 1986). Today, Life has joined other cereals that have jumped on the brand extension bandwagon, with Life Original, Cinnamon, Vanilla, and Pumpkin Spice variations, still in the same original woven rectangle shape.

Photo credit: Wishbook on Flickr.com. Licensed under the Creative Commons Attribution-ShareAlike 2.0 Generic license.

Soda Pop-ular

If you think cereals are old, then soft drinks are positively ancient. The soft drink, probably so named because it contained no "hard" alcohol, is typically comprised of carbonated water (sometimes non-carbonated), flavoring, and a sweetener. Joseph Priestley of England is credited with creating the carbonated water, or soda water, in 1767 that became the core of today's soft drink.

The American soft drink got its start through soda fountains, first appearing in the mid-19th Century, primarily in pharmacies and then at lunch counters. Those soda fountains, of course, may have been how many Boomer kids were first introduced to soft drinks or, at the very least, ice cream sodas. (My personal favorite growing up in New York was the chocolate "egg cream," made from chocolate syrup, soda water, and a splash of milk... no "egg" or "cream" to speak of.) Bottling technology pushed the consumption of soft drinks to new heights.

Coca-Cola and Pepsi-Cola, the two leading brands of American soda (or "pop" in some parts of the country), were both created in drug stores. Atlanta, Georgia pharmacist John Pemberton conceived of a brown carbonated drink with a distinctive taste in 1886. It was named "Coca-Cola" by his partner, Frank Robinson, who also designed the iconic script brand name. Former medical student and New Bern, North Carolina drug store owner Caleb Bradham invented "Brad's Drink" in 1893, renaming it "Pepsi-Cola" in 1898. A little-known fact: Dr Pepper, invented by Charles Alderton, a Waco, Texas pharmacist, was actually conceived in 1885, a year *earlier* than Coca-Cola. In 1929, along came a lemon-lime soda that was one of the first to break away from colas. It had a long, meaningless name that was changed to "7Up" in the 1930s.

Meanwhile, the non-carbonated soft drink category was generally populated by fruit-flavored "-ades" of all kinds. In 1927, Edwin Perkins came up with the Boomer favorite, Kool-Aid (originally spelled "Kool-Ade"). Also in the 1920s, Yoo-hoo, a beverage that qualifies as a chocolate soft drink, was invented by New Jersey grocery store owner Natale Olivieri. It went on to become a national sensation with Boomers.

Why We Loved Soft Drinks

Think of soft drinks as sugar water with tickly bubbles. Who can forget wrapping our meaty little hands around that cold, contoured bottle of Coke and taking a sip of that sweet bubbly, burpy brown beverage? And later during our childhoods, we found that special kind of joy lurking in aluminum cans.

The hard sell of soft drink advertising during the Boomer era was critical to brand-building. Cool slogans abounded. We learned "Things Go Better with Coke" in 1963 and that Coke was "The Real Thing" in 1969. On the other hand, some of us discovered we were actually part of the "Pepsi Generation."

For those of us who were insecure in our younger years, 7Up reassured us in 1952, "You like it… it likes you!" By 1968, 7Up was picking up on our anti-establishment generational angst, calling itself the "Uncola." In the 70s, the Uncola created a raft of Boomer-oriented psychedelic advertising employing the work of pop artist Peter Max. Meanwhile, our more aggressive side found appeal in the 60s slogan of a non-carbonated soft drink: "How about a nice Hawaiian Punch?"

During the 50s, 60s, and 70s, smack dab in the middle of our formative years, soft drinks were in their meteoric ascendancy, and we Boomer kids enthusiastically went along for the ride, craving sugar in liquid form. Cola was to kids what beer was to grown-ups. It was an addiction that surely paved the way for other things. We socialized while we sipped, danced while we downed a glass or two, and grooved while we guzzled. Ah, the refreshing taste of… whatever!

Boomer kids loved another kind of "soft drink" as well – fruit juice. We may very well have first tasted that elixir in a baby bottle. We later learned fruit juice was just a different kind of bottled sugar, not much healthier than soda pop, but no matter. Chances are you had a go-to juice brand as a kid: Maybe Mott's Apple Juice or Welch's Grape Juice.

Some of the popular Boomer era soft drink brands are listed below. Which ones were *your* favorites?

Carbonated

7Up * A&W Root Beer * Coca-Cola * Dr Pepper * Orange Crush * Pepsi-Cola * RC Cola * Tab

Non-carbonated

Hawaiian Punch * Hi-C * Kool-Aid * Mott's Apple Juice * Tang * Welch's Grape Juice * Yoo-hoo

The following trademarks and registered trademarks are the property of their respective holders: 7Up, A&W, Coca-Cola, Coke, Crush, Dr Pepper, Hawaiian Punch, Hi-C, Kool-Aid, Mott, NASA Orange Crush, Pepsi, Pepsi-Cola, Pepsi Generation, RC Cola, Tab, Tang, The Real Thing, Things Go Better with Coke, Uncola, Welch, Yoo-hoo

Sources

https://en.wikipedia.org/wiki/Soft_drink

https://www.worldofcoca-cola.com/about-us/coca-cola-history/

http://www.pepsistore.com/history.asp

https://www.thoughtco.com/history-of-7up-charles-leiper-grigg-4075324

http://kool-aiddays.com/history/

https://www.foodandwine.com/lifestyle/how-nasa-made-tang-cool

http://www.yoo-hoo.com/

http://www.welchsjuice.co.uk/history

https://en.wikipedia.org/wiki/Mott%27s

The Cola Wars

Boomers grew up as the "Cola wars" began to rage. From the very beginning, Coca-Cola and Pepsi-Cola, the number 1 and number 2 colas respectively, duked it out for market share. Coke and Pepsi boasted a similar appearance, logo, bottle, and (some would say) taste. They both strived to capture the heart and soul of Boomer kids through advertising and packaging. It was Pepsi who attempted to co-opt Boomers by first proclaiming them the "Pepsi Generation" in the 60s and then promoting the "Pepsi Challenge" in the 70s. That's when the long-standing rivalry really intensified. By 1985, eroding market share caused Coca-Cola to make one of its few marketing missteps, launching New Coke, a product that changed the formula and failed miserably. Coke had to retrench and reissue the "original" Coke flavor as Coke Classic. 7Up did its part to muddy the waters with its "Uncola" campaign, but that brand never did unseat the two leading colas – nor did Pepsi ever beat out Coke. To this day, Coca-Cola is the top carbonated soft drink in the U.S. and one of the world's best-known, most valued brands.

Photo credit: Pixabay.com

Fruit Juice Frenzy

Dr. Thomas Bramwell Welch is credited with first pasteurizing Concord grape juice in the United States in 1869. His purpose: To offer teetotaler parishioners at a New Jersey church an alternative to sacramental wine. Little did Welch know that Boomer kids would come to worship the Welch's Grape Juice brand as a result. New Yorker Samuel Mott made apple cider in 1842, but it wasn't until 1938 that the Mott's Apple Juice brand was introduced. Both juice brands became Boomer staples. Despite their fruit-based differentiation, Welch's and Mott's certainly competed for mindshare during our childhood. Welch, though, had a leg up in two ways: First, the company also produced Grape Jelly, the essential sweeter half of peanut butter and jelly sandwiches, the most popular Boomer kid sandwich of all time. Second, Welch cleverly hooked up with Disney: In 1955, Welch sponsored the Mickey Mouse Club on television and the company opened a Welch's Grape Juice stand at California's Disneyland, which remained there until 1983.

Photo credit: Grongar on VisualHunt.com. Licensed under the Creative Commons Attribution-ShareAlike 2.0 Generic license.

Tang

Boomers were fascinated with space during our childhood – and Tang became the brand that astronaut John Glenn drank while he circled the Earth in 1962. Tang was an unearthly orange-colored powder invented in 1957 by William Mitchell, a General Foods Corporation food scientist. Add it to water and, presto, you had an unearthly orange-colored Vitamin C-infused breakfast drink. It wasn't a hit with consumers until NASA discovered the stuff when it needed a flavoring to obscure the lousy chemical taste of spaceship water. Tang seemed to fit the bill, so NASA bought the substance in bulk. A blockbuster advertising campaign blasted off as a result of NASA's interest. Tang was pitched as a space-age drink, Glenn as well as other astronauts drank it, and General Foods sponsored television coverage of the Apollo 8 launch in 1968. The brand's sales shot to the moon. While Tang doesn't tingle the tongues of many U.S. kids these days, it remains remarkably popular in Argentina, Brazil, Mexico, and the Middle East. Go figure.

Photo credit: Mike Mozart on Flickr.com. Licensed under the Creative Commons Attribution 2.0 Generic license.

Snack Attack

Americans have long had a love affair with snack foods, but during our Boomer childhood, snacks really skyrocketed in popularity thanks to their natural affinity to television-watching.

Snacks can basically be divided into "sweet" and "salty," spanning a broad range of sub-categories that could easily stand on their own, including candy, cookies and snack cakes, chips and popcorn, chewing gum, and ice cream.

From a Boomer's perspective, candy comprises two groups: "Chocolate" and "all other." The chocolate of our childhood was dominated by two confectionary giants: Hershey and Mars. At the turn of the century, Milton Hershey established a model community to produce chocolate. When you visit Hershey, Pennsylvania today and get a whiff of that delectable confection, you may never want to leave. The eponymous milk chocolate Hershey bar, a 1900 invention, introduced many

Boomer kids to a taste they'd come to love for a lifetime. Frank Mars' first successful chocolate candy bar, Milky Way, was introduced in 1923, followed by Snickers in 1930. But it is those little candy covered chocolate M&Ms, created by Mars in 1945, that Boomers embraced as uniquely theirs.

A classic Boomer candy in the non-chocolate category was PEZ. Invented by Austrian Eduard Haas III in 1927, PEZ didn't arrive in the U.S. until 1952. Perfect timing: PEZ became wildly popular with Boomer kids when fruit flavors were added to the original peppermint flavor. To top it off, the candy was housed in character-themed dispensers. Open wide, Batman!

In the cookies and snack cakes group, Betty Crocker was the reigning queen of the bake-at-home brands. Sorry to burst your bubble, but Betty was nothing more than a fictional character created in the 1940s as an advertising ploy. Packaged cookie favorites of the day included Oreo and Chips Ahoy! brands. In packaged cakes, Hostess dominated with Ding Dongs, Ho Hos, Snoballs, and the ultimate Boomer junk food, Twinkies.

Beloved salt-infested snacks of the 50s and 60s included Lays and Wise potato chips, Fritos corn chips, and salty/sweet old-timer Cracker Jack, promising a prize in every box.

Gum gave Boomer kids something to, um, chew on. The big gorilla in gums, Wrigley, was responsible for such flavors as Doublemint, Spearmint, and Juicy Fruit – all created at the turn of the century but given an advertising boost during the 50s. Even more popular with us kids, though, was bubble gum. The Topps Company's Bazooka bubble gum brand blew into the marketplace in the 1940s.

Say "ice cream" to kids in the 50s and they might very well have answered "Good Humor." Surely one of our favorite sounds was the jingling bell of the Good Humor truck. Howard Johnson's "28 flavors" of ice cream were also magical.

Why We Loved Snacks

Mom may have tried to enforce healthy eating habits, but during the 50s and 60s, snacks burgeoned as a food group. Kids clamored for anything sweet or salty. Snacks nefariously became known as "junk food," a term listed in the 1960 Merriam-Webster Dictionary.

The predominant ingredient in most snacks was, of course, sugar. One cannot under-estimate the effect of sugar coursing through our tiny veins and triggering desire in our little brains. Cereals and soft drinks, combined with snack foods, attacked our digestive and nervous systems with a sugar overload that was nothing short of insidious. There, I said it: Sugar was, and is, something of a food demon. We were already getting high on sugar before we ever discovered the addictive qualities of tobacco, alcohol and drugs. And maybe sex. No wonder little devils of the 50s and 60s hungered for sugar.

Our love of snacks was fueled by media consumption as well, first movies and then television. No Internet, thank you very much. Imagine the total sensory stimulation: Little kids watching and listening to TV while they shoved their hands into wonderful smelling, great tasting, fun feeling junk food. That's a five-sensory fire alarm. And then there was Halloween, the "holiday" we can thank for being the one day of the year when most of us consumed our weight in candy.

Brand promotion contributed mightily to junk food mania. Magazine and television ads enticed kids, as did newspaper cartoon strips and comic books that pitched snack foods. There were legendary tie-ins with children's television programming. More and more grocery shelf space was allotted to snack food brands during the Boomer era. Independent brands were purchased by large food companies and made part of snack food product lines.

Product packaging also got more sophisticated. Snack food bags, boxes, tins and other novel food containers were clearly created to have kid appeal. M&Ms were themselves uniquely designed confections, each a chocolate morsel with a colorful thin candy coating guaranteed to "melt in your mouth, not in your hand." Hostess showed off its luscious little cakes in clear cellophane wrappers, accented with bold primary colors. Cracker Jack, first produced in 1896, didn't appear on television until 1955; its colorful box displayed the product on the outside and offered a prize on the inside – irresistible to us Boomer kids. Pringles put a whole new spin on potato chips by packaging the product in a can instead of the customary bag. And the 1959 introduction of Jiffy Pop boasted a novel self-contained popcorn pan you cooked over a stove (or maybe a campfire). Remember marveling at the rising tin foil?

Some of the popular Boomer era snack brands are listed here. Which ones were *your* favorites?

Sweet
Almond Joy * Bazooka bubble gum * Betty Crocker cookies and cakes *
Cracker Jack * Chips Ahoy! * Ding Dongs * Dubble Bubble bubble gum *
Good Humor * Hershey * Ho Hos * Junior Mints * M&Ms * Oreo * PEZ *
Snoballs * Tic Tacs * Twinkies * Twizzlers

Salty
Cheetos * Cracker Jack * Doritos * EZ Pop * Fritos corn chips * Goldfish *
Jiffy Pop * Lay's potato chips * Planter's Peanuts * Pringles * Wise potato
chips

The following trademarks and registered trademarks are the property of
their respective holders: Almond Joy, Batman, Bazooka, Betty Crocker,
Cheetos, Chips Ahoy!, Cracker Jack, Ding Dongs, Doritos, Dubble Bubble, EZ
Pop, Fleer, Fritos, Goldfish, Good Humor, Ho Hos, Jiffy Pop, Junior Mints,
Lay's, Mars, M&M, Hershey, Howard Johnson, Hostess, Merriam-Webster,
Oreo, PEZ, Planter's, Pringles, Sno Balls, Tic Tacs, Tops, Twinkies, Twizzlers,
Wise, Wrigley's Doublemint, Wrigley's Juicy Fruit, Wrigley's Spearmint

Sources

http://www.candyhistory.net/candy-origin/

https://www.thehersheycompany.com/en_us/home.html

https://www.mars.com/global/about-us/history

https://www.candyfavorites.com/blog/history-of-pez-candy-dispensers/

https://en.wikipedia.org/wiki/Twizzlers

http://www.pbs.org/food/the-history-kitchen/who-was-betty-crocker/

https://www.seriouseats.com/2017/08/history-of-oreos-bravetart-
cookbook.html

http://www.hostessbrands.com/phoenix.zhtml?c=254431&p=irol-irhome

https://en.wikipedia.org/wiki/Twinkie

http://www.wisesnacks.com/our-history/

https://www.fritolay.com/get-to-know-us/company

http://www.softschools.com/inventions/history/bubble_gum_history/362/

https://www.oldtimecandy.com/discontinued/bazooka-bubble-gum/

https://www.foodandwine.com/news/how-gum-and-baseball-cards-became-intertwined

http://www.goodhumor.com/article

https://www.barrypopik.com/index.php/new_york_city/entry/junk_food/

 **Bubble Gum**

Frank Fleer, the founder of the Fleer Chewing Gum Company, invented the first bubble gum as early as 1906, but it couldn't be commercially produced. Walter Diemer did some experimenting for Fleer and in 1928, he created a bubble gum with the right consistency. It was pink because that was the color of food dye Fleer had the most of at the time. The company called it Dubble Bubble. Diemer tested the product at a candy store and 100 pieces sold out in a day. The more popular Boomer bubble gum, though, was Bazooka, created in 1947 by the Topps Company. It was named after a musical instrument. Each bite-sized, wrapped package of the also pink gum carried a tiny comic strip about a character with an eye patch named "Bazooka Joe." Bubble gum survived in another form (flat) when it was packaged with baseball cards in 1952.

Photo credit: Pixabay.com

Good Humor

In 1920, confectioner Harry Burt of Ohio came up with a chocolate coating he could wrap around ice cream. He added a wooden handle and created the first Good Humor bar. His patent was granted three years later when he showed up at the Patent Office in Washington, D.C. with Good Humor bars for officials to try. Deliciously smart move, Harry. In the 20s, a person's "humor" meant his temperament, hence the brand name. Burt's ice cream innovation was all the more remarkable because he decided to sell the bars from trucks outfitted with freezers and bells. Product expansion followed, and kids followed the trucks. Good Humor trucks and their drivers became so popular nationally that a feature film, "The Good Humor Man," was made in 1950. Good Humor abandoned its fleet of trucks in the 70s to focus on retail sales. Today, the Good Humor brand still exists, being sold in grocery stores, from city pushcarts, and from an occasional leftover Good Humor truck.

Photo credit: Kim Scarborough on VisualHunt.com. Licensed under the Creative Commons Attribution 2.0 Generic license.

Oreo

Oreos were produced in 1912 by the National Biscuit Company (Nabisco), but the brand was re-launched as the "new Oreos" in the 50s. Oreo represents a rare case of a number 2 brand knocking off a number 1 brand. Oreo was actually a copycat, a direct competitor of Hydrox, a chocolate wafer-and-cream sandwich cookie invented years before Oreo and produced by the Loose-Wiles Biscuit Company, later renamed Sunshine Biscuits. Hydrox, with its beautifully adorned outside wafers, was a smash hit early on. Oreo wasn't. But Loose-Wiles made the mistake of not protecting its brand name, and "Hydrox" was appended to a raft of products, including chemicals. The company never changed the name, trying to promote Hydrox as the "original" chocolate wafer cookie and warning in its ads, "Don't be fooled by look-alikes!" It didn't work: Hydrox eventually flopped. Oreo, meanwhile, advertised its goodness, captured the top spot, and went on to become a Boomer Brand favorite. Today, Oreo comes in various iterations of flavor and size and remains the king of cookies.

Photo credit: Pixabay.com

Twinkies

In 1919, the Hostess CupCake was introduced by Continental Baking Company. That was the beginning of a long line of Hostess brand snack cakes. Twinkies were created in 1930 by baking manager James Dewar. He conceived of Twinkies when strawberries were out of season and a machine used to make cream-filled strawberry shortcake had nothing better to do. He made up the name upon seeing a billboard for "Twinkle Toe Shoes," so the story goes. Dewar used bananas to make a cream filling for sponge cake, fired up the idle machine, and Twinkies were born. When bananas were rationed during World War II, Twinkies became vanilla cream-filled. Later, other flavors were added. A Twinkie was the ultimate Boomer junk food: It was celebrated in movies, on television, in songs, and even appeared as a deep-fried confection at state fairs. Sadly, the maker of Twinkies filed for bankruptcy in 2012 and Boomers thought it was lights out for Twinkies. But the Hostess brand family has since re-emerged. The irresistible sweet treat is being churned out once more, so all is well in Twinkieland.

Photo credit: Pixabay.com

Faster Foods

Until the 50s and 60s came along, mom, whose responsibilities included captaining the family meals, pretty much had to make everything from scratch. It was laborious and time-consuming. Those clever companies in the food business smelled a sea change when the post-World War II population in the United States spiked. Clearly, mom needed some help in the kitchen, and that's when convenience foods took off, all in an effort to make it easier and faster to fix breakfast, lunch and especially dinner.

Not that convenience foods didn't exist before. For example, Campbell's introduced tomato soup in a can as early as 1895. It advertised soups on radio using the jingle "M'm, M'm Good!" in 1931. But in 1941, after expanding its soup line, the company opened Campbell's Test Kitchens to develop recipes that used the company's condensed soups. (Aha! Now you know how that "green bean mushroom casserole" mom made came to be).

Campbell's is just one example of the mid-20th Century explosion in bagged, bottled, boxed, canned, frozen, and otherwise "prepared" foods. Some convenience foods already existed but became Boomer staples, such as Kraft Macaroni & Cheese, first introduced as a Depression-era product. Believe it or not, the peanut butter and jelly sandwich wasn't a Boomer invention either; there is a reference to such a concoction as early as 1901. But Boomer kids popularized PB&J. Not only did it taste so darn good, the three basic ingredients – peanut butter, jelly, and sliced white bread – were all easily and cheaply available in packaged form during our childhood. In 1968, Smucker's made it even easier to craft a PB&J sandwich with the introduction of Goober, a combination of peanut butter *and* jelly in a jar.

Perhaps the seminal example of fast, convenient food, was the Swanson TV dinner, introduced in 1954. The name alone tells us just how embedded television was in American family life. The mother of invention for this product was a turkey – actually, 260 tons of turkey that Swanson & Sons was stuck with, surely the world's record for Thanksgiving leftovers. What to do, what to do? Gerry Thomas, a Swanson salesman, found inspiration in airline food trays, and tons of turkey were turned into trays of ready-made turkey dinners. Swanson sold ten million of these all-in-one meals in the first year. They switched to paper trays when the microwave oven became a consumer favorite – but by then, Swanson had started a whole class of ready-made meals that remains popular in the frozen foods section of today's grocery stores.

Why We Loved Convenience Foods

As with cereals, soft drinks, and snacks, convenience foods often contained that magical substance, sugar, but it wasn't nearly as prominent or obvious an ingredient. From a Boomer kid perspective, taste, texture, and smell were all important – and so was the fact that a meal could be made fast. Even a kid could make a carb-loaded PB&J sandwich in a jiffy.

Faster lunches, yummier dinners, more time to watch television or play outside… whatever the reasons, Boomer kids loved convenience food brands. Actually, we may not have even realized they were "brands." "B&M" became synonymous with baked beans, "Campbell's" with soup, "Heinz" with ketchup, "Skippy" with peanut butter, "Welch's" with grape jelly, and "Wonder" with bread. In many cases, one brand dominated the market early on to define an entire product category.

There were always clever attempts to differentiate a brand and appeal to kids, especially when competition was stiff. In 1961, for example, borrowing from cereal mascots, StarKist introduced a cartoon mascot, Charlie the Tuna. In television commercials, the hapless tuna always heard the phrase, "Sorry Charlie," because he just wasn't good enough to get himself caught so he could be canned by StarKist. We kids may not have understood the whole logic behind "Why would a tuna *want* to be caught?" but that didn't really matter. If we liked tuna fish, we probably wanted mom to buy StarKist Tuna, largely because of Charlie.

Convenience food brand marketers knew where to reach Boomer kids – on television, of course. That's why in 1950,

Campbell's not only advertised on television, it sponsored such popular shows as "Lassie." Other brands followed suit. You'd often find TV personalities (both live and animated) endorsing convenience food products.

These brands also used ingenious packaging and promotions to make sure they connected with us. Convenience foods found unique ways to enter our psyches. Some examples include:

- the elevation of a common fruit to stardom through the 1944 creation of Chiquita Banana
- the 1952 Oscar Mayer Wienermobile that toured the country to promote the brand's hot dogs
- the brilliantly named Pop-Tarts toaster pastries which, according to Kellogg's, appropriated the popularity of "Pop-Art" in the 60s.

Some of the popular Boomer era convenience food brands are listed below. Which ones were *your* favorites?

B&M Baked Beans * Campbell's Soups * Cheez Whiz * Chiquita Bananas * Fluff * Heinz Ketchup * Heinz Pickles * Jell-O * Jif Peanut Butter * Kraft Macaroni & Cheese * Mott's Apple Sauce * Nestle * Quik * Oscar Mayer hot dogs * Ovaltine * Pop-Tarts * Skippy Peanut Butter * Smucker's Goober * SpaghettiOs * StarKist Tuna * Swanson's TV Dinners * Welch's Grape Jelly * Wonder Bread

Sources

https://www.campbells.com/campbell-history/

https://www.smithsonianmag.com/arts-culture/marvelous-macaroni-and-cheese-30954740/

https://www.lovepbj.com/

https://www.seriouseats.com/2007/04/the-history-of-the-peanut-butt.html

https://www.smithsonianmag.com/history/tray-bon-96872641/

https://en.wikipedia.org/wiki/StarKist

https://en.wikipedia.org/wiki/Wienermobile

https://www.chiquita.com/discover/miss-chiquita

https://www.foodandwine.com/fwx/food/not-so-american-history-cheez-whiz

http://www.jellogallery.org/history.html

https://www.chronicallyvintage.com/2015/10/adventures-in-vintage-advertising-jell.html

https://gizmodo.com/the-fascinating-untold-history-of-jell-o-1508125288

https://recipereminiscing.wordpress.com/2016/10/06/the-history-of-ovaltine/

https://en.wikipedia.org/wiki/Nesquik

Cheez Whiz

Cheese and wine may be a natural together, but there is also a long and celebrated history of the pairing of cheese and children. It's no wonder, then, that cheese was a fundamentally important food to most Boomer kids. Not surprisingly, though, it was processed cheese that we liked best (think salt). Kraft's introduction of the processed cheese slice (the Kraft Single) in 1950 gave many of us the easy cheesy product we loved. That little invention turned "grilled cheese" sandwiches into its own food group. For those of us who weren't happy with cheese unless it was truly gooey, Kraft struck gold again with Cheez Whiz in 1953. This processed cheese in a jar was actually introduced a year earlier by Kraft in the United Kingdom as a pre-packaged cheese sauce to modernize the Brits' famous Welsh rarebit. The product was so popular there it debuted the next year in the United States. And yes, you can still buy it.

Photo credit: VelcrO on VisualHunt.com. Licensed under the Creative Commons Attribution 2.0 Generic license.

Jell-O

Jell-O's jiggles were one of its more remarkable qualities. The Jell-O brand was basically gelatin, which goes back thousands of years, but the fruit flavored powdery stuff was first created in 1897 as a dessert. In the early 1900s, an aggressive sales force, combined with magazine advertising promoting free recipe books and samples, forged the road to Jell-O's success. By 1934, General Foods' Jell-O brand was being advertised on radio with the help of Jack Benny. That's when everyone learned how to spell J-E-L-L-O. The 40s and 50s saw Jell-O's emergence as a nifty mold-maker; "Jell-O salad" became synonymous with holiday side dishes, even if purists still preferred it as an unaltered dessert. Ads of the 50s advised us, "Now's the time for Jell-O." When the brand started to decline in the late 60s and early 70s, it was rejuvenated via television advertising. Ads starred comedian Bill Cosby who, for over thirty years, helped keep Jell-O relevant. That campaign is believed to be the longest running celebrity endorsement in advertising history.

Photo credit: Mike Mozart on Flickr.com. Licensed under the Creative Commons Attribution 2.0 Generic license.

Ovaltine

Milk wasn't usually a preferred Boomer beverage. Thankfully, it could be modified and made quite a bit tastier with a chocolate powder additive, Ovaltine. This strangely named substance was first made in Switzerland under the name "Ovomaltine," which combined the Latin word for egg (ovum) and malt, two of its original ingredients. A misspelling in an early English trademark application created "Ovaltine." It caught on with Boomers when the product was advertised on the "Captain Midnight" radio show in the 40s, and then the television show in the 50s. In one of the most effective children's television tie-ins ever, Captain Midnight (actor Richard Webb) offered to send a membership kit and "secret decoder ring" to kids who collected proofs of purchase from Ovaltine jars and mailed them in. Nestle Quik, a competitive chocolate milk flavoring powder, was introduced in 1948. That brand employed a ventriloquist in 1955 TV commercials, ending with the tag line: "N-E-S-T-L-E-S, Nestle's makes the very best... Chocolate!"

Photo credit: Arnold Gatilao on Flickr.com. Licensed under the Creative Commons Attribution 2.0 Generic license.

Playtime

Leisure time became an increasingly important component of American life during the 50s and 60s. Families were beginning to realize that there was more to everyday living than collecting a paycheck and making mortgage payments. Boomer kids discovered that doing odd jobs during their free time could result in "allowance," remuneration that, while small, enabled them to buy stuff to enjoy during playtime. They were also indulged by their parents, who didn't hesitate to amuse their kids with toys and games.

Boomer kids had no shortage of opportunities to take advantage of leisure time, whether it was watching television, adventuring outside, or playing with games and toys indoors. While there was plenty of time to spend with friends, time with family was important, too – families watched television together, played games together, and took vacations together (often road trips).

As a form of entertainment, television itself opened up an entire world to kids. After all, back then there were no computers, cell phones, video games or Internet. As noted earlier, television also became a major thoroughfare for advertising all kinds of products to children, from cereals, to snacks and soft drinks, to toys and games. Later, television catered to our love of music as well.

Companies such as Fisher-Price, Hasbro, Mattel, Milton Bradley and Parker Brothers recognized that playtime was serious business, flooding the market with toy and game brands that became classics. In fact, many of our childhood playtime favorites still exist today. Wham-O specialized in fads, producing wildly popular toy brands, such as Frisbee and Hula Hoop.

Some Americans believe the first real commercialization of Christmas was due to the 1930s interpretation of Santa Claus in Coca-Cola advertising. As a gift-giving holiday, though, parents of the Boomer era really popularized Christmas. They took commercializing Christmas to an extreme, often lavishing gifts upon their kids during the holiday seasons of the 50s and 60s. That's why it's likely many of the toy and game brands we fondly remember first came into our lives when they found their way under the family Christmas tree.

Why We Loved Playtime Brands

Playtime gave us a sense of freedom and adventure. It was a respite from school and around-the-house responsibilities. "Go out and play" were words we anxiously waited to hear – that was one parental directive we never challenged.

Outdoors, our playtime was enhanced with Frisbees we could throw, Hula Hoops we could gyrate with, Schwinn bikes we could ride, and WIFFLE Balls we could hit. We raced down sidewalks with various brands of roller skates, most of which required keys to tighten them onto our shoes. We pulled along our friends, or maybe our dogs, in those trusty red Radio Flyer wagons. We hurtled down snow-covered hills on our Flexible Flyer sleds.

Indoors, we loved playing board games with family and friends – Candyland when we were younger, the Game of Life, Monopoly, Risk and Scrabble when we were older. Twister made it easy for us to achieve a little innocent intimacy as adolescent boys and girls.

We built Revell models of cars, ships, and planes. We had wonderful toys to keep us busy for hours as we grew up – Barbie dolls to dress, GI Joe action figures to do battle, LEGO to build, Matchbox cars to race, Lionel trains to navigate around tracks, and Silly Putty to do just about anything with. Action Comics and DC Comics encouraged us to fantasize. Little Golden Books taught us to read. Classics Illustrated made us appreciate classic tales. MAD magazine fueled our rebelliousness and kept us laughing.

Television was a pastime if not an addiction for us kids. We loved Westerns starring such character "brands" as the Lone Ranger, Paladin, the Rifleman, Rin Tin Tin and Wyatt Earp; cartoons and shows featuring super heroes like Batman and Superman; and we couldn't get enough of anything with the Disney name attached to it.

Technology during our childhood was different from today but just as marvelous. Our amazement never waned when we experienced 3-D images seen through a View-Master or witnessed instant photographs pop out of a Polaroid camera. And color television... that just blew our minds.

Some of the popular Boomer era toys, games and comics are listed below. Which ones were *your* favorites?

Action Comics * Aurora models * Barbie * Candyland * Careers * Chatty Cathy * Classics Illustrated * DC Comics * Etch A Sketch * Flexible Flyer * Frisbee * Game of Life * GI Joe * Hot Wheels * Hula Hoop * LEGO * Lincoln Logs * Lionel Trains * Little Golden Books * MAD Magazine * Matchbox Cars * Monopoly * Mouse Trap * Operation * Play Doh * Mr. Potato Head * Polaroid * Radio Flyer * Revell models * Risk * Schwinn * Scrabble * Silly Putty * Slinky * Stratego * Tiddly Winks * Tiny Tears * Twister * View-Master * WIFFLE Ball

The following trademarks and registered trademarks are the property of their respective holders: Action Comics, Aurora, Barbie, Batman, Candyland, Careers, Chatty Cathy, Coca-Cola, Classics Illustrated, Concentration, DC Comics, Disney, Etch A Sketch, FAST COMPANY, Fisher-Price, Flexible Flyer, Frisbee, Game of Life, GI Joe, Hasbro, Hot Wheels, Hula Hoop, LEGO, LEGOLAND, Lincoln Logs, Lionel, Lone Ranger, Macy's, MAD, Matchbox, Milton Bradley, Monopoly, Mouse Trap, Mr. Potato Head, Operation, Polaroid, Pop-o-Matic, Radio Flyer, Revell, Rifleman, Rin Tin Tin, Risk, Schwinn, Scrabble, Silly Putty, Slinky, Stratego, Superman, Tiddly Winks, Trouble, Twister, View-Master, Wham-O, WIFFLE Ball, Yahtzee

Sources

https://www.lego.com/en-us/aboutus/lego-group/the_lego_history

https://www.fastcompany.com/3040223/when-it-clicks-it-clicks

https://www.legoland.com/about/

https://en.wikipedia.org/wiki/Mad_(magazine)

https://www.madmagazine.com/

http://www.wiffle.com/pages/welcome.asp?page=welcome

https://en.wikipedia.org/wiki/Wiffle_ball

Board Games

What made board games so popular in the 50s and 60s? It was kind of the perfect playtime storm. There was a growing audience in families who had leisure time to spend together. Kids were enthralled with visual and tactile experiences. Complex game boards and paraphernalia could be created at reasonable prices. Disney characters and movies, comic book super heroes and popular television shows contributed to board game tie-ins. The 50s saw the introduction of Candyland, the reintroduction of Scrabble (a 1930s game popularized when Macy's started selling it in 1952), the Disney movie tie-in Peter Pan adventure game, the more serious-minded Careers, and the battle game Risk. In the 60s, gaming sophistication spiked with the Game of Life (an update of an 1860 game), the army game Stratego, Mouse Trap (easy to play but hard to set up), Trouble and Operation, a skill game that may have launched surgical careers. The 60s also saw the inception of board games mimicking TV game shows, such as Concentration. Despite the advent of video games, board games remain popular today.

Photo credit: Pixabay.com

 LEGO

One of a small number of non-American Boomer Brands, LEGO is an abbreviation of two Danish words, "leg" and "godt," meaning "play well." LEGO got its start in the small workshop of a Danish carpenter, Ole Kirk Kristiansen. In 1932, he founded the LEGO Group to make wooden and plastic toys. In the 1940s, the company manufactured their tiny "bricks," but in 1958 the current plastic version of the LEGO brick was introduced. The "stub-and-tube" coupling system of the LEGO brick is unique and patented. A timeless toy, LEGO is the favorite of millions of children around the world, and it has twice been named "Toy of the Century." LEGO Group has been ranked by the Reputation Institute as the second most highly regarded company in the world. LEGO has leveraged its brand to produce other toy brands, LEGO movies, and even LEGOLAND – LEGO-themed entertainment parks, accompanied by LEGOLAND Hotels. *FAST COMPANY* called LEGO "a profit-generating, design-driven miracle built around premium, intuitive, highly covetable hardware that fans can't get enough of."

Photo credit: Kelly Sikemma on Unsplash.com

MAD

Launched in 1952, MAD was a satire and parody magazine. It famously poked fun at issues far and wide, becoming notorious for parodies of television, movies, music and politics. In challenging authority and lampooning American society, the magazine quickly became a favorite of Boomers. Sometimes hysterically funny and often in extremely poor taste, MAD lambasted and lacerated just about every aspect of American life. The magazine was also unique because it declined to accept advertising for the most part, primarily so that it could parody advertising campaigns. In pushing the boundaries, MAD found itself subject to legal actions, even appearing before the Supreme Court in 1961. That's when music publishers filed a copyright infringement suit against MAD for parodying songs by such famous composers as Irving Berlin, Cole Porter and Richard Rogers. MAD won the case. Despite numerous changes to the magazine's staff, MAD, featuring the iconic mascot Alfred E. Neuman, is still being published today.

Photo credit: Smabs Sputzer on VisualHunt.com. Licensed under the Creative Commons Attribution 2.0 Generic license.

WIFFLE Ball

In 1953, a young boy and his friend were batting around a perforated golf ball in their Connecticut backyard. His father, David Mullany, got the idea to create a baseball-size plastic ball with perforations that wouldn't break windows and would be easy to curve when it was thrown. Because it caused kids to strike out a lot, or "wiff," the ball was named the WIFFLE Ball. According to The WIFFLE Ball's website, after experimentation, a ball with eight oblong cut-outs worked the best: "To this day, we don't know exactly why it works...it just does!!" Boomer kids loved the baseball alternative in the 60s, and a World WIFFLE Ball Championship was established in 1980. The WIFFLE Balls and accompanying plastic bats continue to be sold all over the U.S. and in other countries as well. In 2017, the WIFFLE Ball was inducted into the National Toy Hall of Fame, the criteria for which is a toy known for icon status, longevity, discovery and innovation.

Photo credit: Jeepers Media on VisualHunt.com. Licensed under the Creative Commons Attribution 2.0 Generic license.

The Dazzle of Disney

The Disney brand has had such a huge influence on the Boomer generation that it is wholly deserving of singular attention. Walt Disney was an extraordinary visionary who admitted the founding of The Walt Disney Company was really due to an animated mouse, namely Mickey Mouse. Disney started out as an animator, and Disney's early cartoon characters in the 1920s – Mickey Mouse joined by Pluto, Goofy, and Donald Duck – first garnered attention from children. But it was "Snow White and the Seven Dwarfs," the 1937 feature-length animated film, that revolutionized animation, was beloved by children, and achieved worldwide success for Walt Disney.

The 40s and 50s saw the production of a raft of animated films that further enhanced Disney's reputation, including "Alice in Wonderland," "Bambi," "Cinderella," "Fantasia," and "Peter Pan." Also at this time, Disney moved into live-action films, one of which was the visually exotic and popular "20,000

Leagues Under the Sea," released in 1954. These early films set the tone for cinematic innovation and excellence that would become Disney trademarks in subsequent decades.

Not surprisingly, Walt Disney also discovered the power of television. He perfectly leveraged the new medium to appeal to Boomer kids. In 1955, Disney launched the Mickey Mouse Club on television, a show for children, with children as the stars. The group of "Mouseketeers" were led by "Head Mousketeer" Jimmie Dodd, an adult. "M-I-C-K-E-Y (Why? Because we love you!) M-O-U-S-E" was the theme song all Boomer kids recognized. The original Mickey Mouse Club ran on the ABC television network until 1958. Coincidentally, the Walt Disney Company acquired ABC decades later.

Disney's foray into family programming on television began with the launch of another of Walt's personal dreams, Disneyland, which opened in California in 1955. He used TV to feature the new theme park, its rides and attractions. "Walt Disney's Disneyland" (1954 – 1958) was the forerunner of several more TV shows, all built around Disney entertainment in the broadest sense: "Walt Disney Presents" (1958 – 1961), the color TV-oriented "Walt Disney's Wonderful World of Color" (1961 – 1969), and "The Wonderful World of Disney" (1969 – 1979 and 1991 – present). Walt himself was the host of Disney TV programs; his friendly, folksy visage became widely known to kids and their parents throughout the country. Some of these shows featured episodes that became individually popular and took on lives of their own, such as Davy Crockett and Daniel Boone. Disney brilliantly marketed the Davy Crockett and Daniel

Boone characters, producing hats and other related merchandise. Actor Fess Parker played Davy Crockett in multiple episodes. (In 1964, a Daniel Boone television show not associated with Disney aired for over five years. It starred none other than Fess Parker.)

Disney's first theme park, Disneyland, opened up a whole new avenue for attracting children and their families to the Disney brand, as well as for Disney merchandising. In the first ten years of Disneyland's operation, fifty million visitors passed through its gates. That led to the development of Disney World in Orlando, Florida in 1965, a year before Walt Disney's death. Disney World officially opened in 1971.

The venerable Walt Disney Company has reinvented itself over and over with astounding results: Disney has gone on to become the world's largest independent media conglomerate in terms of revenue.

Why We Loved Disney

Walt Disney himself seemed to be the kid who never grew up. He had an innate sense of what would appeal to kids and didn't hesitate to turn his dreams into reality. The height of Disney's creativity occurred during the period Boomer kids were growing up. Any time Disney launched something, whether it was cartoons, films, television shows or theme parks, we were all ready to pledge our allegiance to Disney.

We loved Disney cartoons, Disney films, Disney toys, Disney collectibles, Disney properties. How could we not? We were the ideal audience for anything and everything Disney.

Chances are many of us not only watched and joined the Mickey Mouse Club, we *felt like* one of the Mouseketeers. When it came to Disney's night-time television entertainment, we surely made it a point to sit down and watch "Uncle Walt" with our families, much as we all watched the Ed Sullivan Show. The Disney merchandising machine was just as adept at movie and television tie-ins; whether it was Mousketeer hats, action figures, stuffed toys, or movie DVDs, we probably owned Disney stuff as kids and bought Disney stuff as adults for *our* kids and grandkids.

It would have been a rare treat during our childhoods to visit Disneyland in California – but even if we didn't, as adults we probably wangled our way to visit Disneyland or Disney World in Florida with our own children. I went to Disney World with my wife and daughter. We also took our daughter on a Disney Cruise, a remarkably well-run operation that only served to further enhance our positive perception of the Disney brand. And what a brand it is: Disney is that rare company that consistently surpasses your expectations.

We grew up with Disney and formed a lasting relationship with Disney. We have passed along our love of all things Disney to our children – and probably to our grandchildren. We're not just the Boomer generation – we're the Disney generation.

The following trademarks and registered trademarks are the property of their respective holders: ABC, Disney, Disneyland, Disney World, Donald Duck, Goofy, Imagineer, Mickey Mouse, Mickey Mouse Club, Minnie Mouse, Mouseketeer, Pluto, Walt Disney

Sources

https://en.wikipedia.org/wiki/The_Walt_Disney_Company

https://studioservices.go.com/disneystudios/history.html

https://en.wikipedia.org/wiki/The_Mickey_Mouse_Club

https://www.npr.org/templates/story/story.php?storyId=130979892

http://www.originalmmc.com/cast.html

http://www.justdisney.com/disneyland/history.html

https://metv.com/stories/remembering-the-wonderful-world-of-disney

https://en.wikipedia.org/wiki/Walt_Disney_anthology_television_series

http://disney.wikia.com/wiki/Mickey_Mouse_Ears_Hat

https://en.wikipedia.org/wiki/Walt_Disney_Parks_and_Resorts

https://disneyparks.disney.go.com/blog/2011/09/timeline-celebrating-40-years-at-walt-disney-world/

https://waltdisney.org/blog/selling-mickey-rise-disney-marketing

 Mickey Mouse Ears

The "Mickey Mouse Ears" black felt hat got its start with the Mouseketeers on the Mickey Mouse Club. The inspiration for the hat came to Disney employee Roy Williams, who saw Mickey tip his ears to Minnie Mouse in the 1929 cartoon, "The Karnival Kid." Williams himself appeared on the Mickey Mouse Club show. All of the Mouseketeers, including adult host Jimmie Dodd, wore Mickey Mouse Ears. Reportedly, out of the ten million kids who watched the Mickey Mouse Club in its first season, two million Mickey Mouse Ears hats were snapped up in the first three months. The Mickey Mouse Club was revived several times through 1996. As of 2017, it was still airing under the name Club Mickey Mouse, but exclusively on social media. Mickey Mouse Ears have always been prominent on the show. The Mickey Mouse Ears hat remains by far the most popular souvenir purchased at Disney parks and resorts.

Photo credit: Sam Howzit on VisualHunt.com. Licensed under the Creative Commons Attribution 2.0 Generic license.

Disney Parks and Resorts

Disney theme parks aren't just amusement parks. They are worlds of their own conceived by Disney Imagineers. The visionary Walt Disney executed a completely different form of family entertainment when he developed Disneyland in the mid-50s. In 1965, Walt Disney proposed his grandest vision yet, Disney World, which debuted in Florida in 1971, five years after his death. Disney World eclipsed Disneyland in size and scope; it is surrounded by Disney Resort hotels and has continued to expand since its opening. Disney World has been followed by other Disney properties nationally and worldwide, including Disneyland Paris, the Hong Kong Disneyland Resort, the Shanghai Disney Resort, the Tokyo Disney Resort, and Disney Cruises. In addition to innovative, one-of-a-kind entertainment at these properties, superb customer service is part of the Disney experience.

Photo credit: Pixabay.com

 **Disney Merchandising**

According to The Walt Disney Family Museum, Walt Disney first recognized the potential of merchandising in 1929, when he was offered $300 for the right to feature Mickey Mouse on a children's writing tablet. The tablet was a success, and the concept of merchandising Disney characters was born. As with everything Disney himself touched, however, he made sure that any deals executed were in support of only high-quality merchandise. By the 1930s, Mickey and Minnie Mouse found their names and images on everything from wallpaper to clothing. Perhaps one of the most famous Disney items ever produced was the Mickey Mouse watch. On the first day of the timepiece's introduction in 1933, 11,000 Mickey Mouse watches were sold at Macy's in New York. Today, Mickey Mouse watches are treasured collectibles. Disney merchandise of all kinds continues to be produced and sold globally through Disney Parks, Disney Resorts, Disney Stores, and through many other retail outlets.

Photo credit: Tombird1 on Flickr.com. Licensed under the Creative Commons Attribution 2.0 Generic license.

Lookin' Good, Feelin' Good

Looking and feeling good in the 50s and 60s was associated with style, modernity and affluence. Growing up, Boomer girls were likely to be fascinated by the face powder, eye liner and lipstick their moms applied, and by the rollers their moms wore in their hair, before going out on a special occasion. Likewise, Boomer boys watched with amazement as their dads whisked off their beards with razors and then splashed their faces with after-shave lotion. These rituals were part of a post-World War II American culture that put a premium on one's appearance.

Visual images of the era surrounding our parents and ourselves reinforced the notion of looking good, particularly in the 50s. On the big screen, Hollywood movie stars began to appear in vivid color, wearing hairstyles, makeup and clothing that enchanted the average American. Fashion and cosmetics companies took advantage of women's aspirations, producing such breakthrough beauty brands as Revlon's Fire & Ice, a lip-stick/nail enamel combination that caused a sensation in 1952, and Clairol, a brand that thought to ask the daring question, "Does she... or doesn't she?" in its breakthrough hair coloring campaign of 1956. Women and men "dressed up" when they appeared in public; men in white-collar positions were expected to wear suits and ties to work.

While it may seem strange today, cigarettes were an integral part of looking good back then. Smoking cigarettes was widely accepted in the American culture of the 50s and 60s; it was considered socially sophisticated and even sexy to smoke. Smoking was legitimized in movies by both male and female actors. Cigarettes were just as prominent on television: Renowned newscaster Edward R. Murrow and Tonight Show host Jack Paar both smoked on television. Celebrities routinely endorsed cigarette brands. Some cigarette brand advertising in the 50s even promoted the health benefits of tobacco. And Marlboro added a new macho quality to smoking when it reoriented its brand, originally for women, into a brand for men with the highly successful "Marlboro Country" campaign. Cigarettes were among the most heavily advertised and popular brands during our childhood.

When looking good meshed with feeling good, great things happened for a brand. A prime example of this was the introduction of Procter & Gamble's Crest toothpaste in 1955. Until then, toothpastes were only cosmetic; Crest, however, was cosmetic *and* therapeutic. The first toothpaste to contain stannous fluoride, Crest used extensive product trials to prove its effectiveness in fighting cavities. That led to Crest gaining the American Dental Association's endorsement in 1960, before any other toothpaste. Crest's market share went from less than 9 percent in 1958 to more than 30 percent by 1962.

Why We Loved Brands that Made Us Look and Feel Good

As pre-adolescent youngsters, most Boomer kids emulated their parents. Remember those early photographs of you and your siblings, dressed up to look like little moms and dads? Your hair was neat, your teeth were white, and your Buster Browns or Mary Janes were shiny. You had on either a handsome button-down shirt or a lovely little dress. During playtime, though, you were more likely to wear jeans and Keds.

You may have brushed your teeth with Ipana (Bucky Beaver, a Disney character, was its mascot), but you were just as likely to use Pepsodent or Colgate; that is, before your mom switched to Crest. As an adolescent boy, you may have used Brylcreem because, "A little dab'll do ya." As an adolescent girl, you may have carefully washed your face with Palmolive soap, shampooed your hair with Prell, and used a new product, Secret deodorant, for the very first time.

Looking good as little kids was not nearly as important as looking good as adolescents, when we discovered the opposite sex. That's when clean fingernails, combed hair (slicked back for the guys in the 50s), sweet-smelling breath, and a distinct lack of body odor were essential to attracting the girl or boy of our dreams. Adolescent boys may have even used a little of dad's after-shave, and girls may have added a little something extra to their bras. Right about then is when we really discovered the brands that enhanced our appearance.

Of course, everything changed in the turbulent 60s. A cultural fault line appeared as our generation split in two, with brand preferences following suit. On one side were the more conventional Boomer teens and young adults, to whom "looking good" meant modeling their appearance after the traditional adult men and women of the 60s. On the other side were the anti-establishment Boomers. For them, looking good may have meant adopting the London-inspired "Mod" look – stylish and hip. Or, it may have meant dispensing with looking good altogether, instead embracing the long hair, bell bottom jeans, bare feet, beads and drug paraphernalia of the counter-culture.

Some of the popular Boomer era health, beauty and clothing brands are listed below. Which ones do *you* remember?
Brylcreem * Buster Brown * Clairol * Clearasil * Colgate * Coppertone * Crest * Dove * Ice O Derm * Ipana * Keds * Levi's * Mary Janes * Mennen * Old Spice * Palmolive * Pepsodent * Prell * Revlon's Fire & Ice * Secret * Thom McAn

Cigarette Brands

Many cigarette brands pre-dated Boomers, but their popularity grew throughout the Boomer era. You may have snuck a cigarette or two from your parents or older siblings. Or maybe you got hold of one from a friend, surreptitiously took a puff or two behind the school building, and promptly coughed your lungs out. Which of these cigarette brands did your parents favor – and which of them did *you* try as a kid?

Benson & Hedges * Camel * Chesterfield * Kent * Kool * L&M * Lucky Strike * Marlboro * Pall Mall * Parliament * Salem * Tareyton * Virginia Slims * Winston

The following trademarks and registered trademarks are the property of their respective holders: American Bandstand, Benson & Hedges, Brylcreem, Bucky Beaver, Buster Brown, Camel, Cheerios, Chesterfield, Clairol, Clearasil, Colgate, Coppertone, Crest, Disney, Dove, Enovid, Ice O Derm, Ipana, Keds, Kent, Kool, L&M, Levi's, Lucky Strike, Marlboro, Mary Janes, Mennen, Old Spice, Pall Mall, Palmolive, Parliament, Pepsodent, Planned Parenthood, Prell, Revlon's Fire & Ice, Salem, Secret, Tareyton, Thom McAn Virginia Slims, Winston You've Come a Long Way, Baby

Sources

http://www.fashionthrill.com/2013/09/revlons-fire-ice-and-cherries-in-snow.html

https://hbswk.hbs.edu/archive/how-crest-made-business-history

http://glamourdaze.com/history-of-makeup/1950s

http://www.lipstickandcurls.net/blog/1950s-make-up-a-look-at-popular-beauty-brands-from-the-era/

http://hair-and-makeup-artist.com/womens-1960s-makeup/

https://www.nytimes.com/2007/03/20/health/20essay.html

https://americacomesalive.com/2016/06/20/buster-brown-shoes-mary-janes/

https://www.keds.com/en/about-us/

https://en.wikipedia.org/wiki/Keds_(shoes)

https://oureverydaylife.com/the-history-of-coppertone-12210796.html

https://en.wikipedia.org/wiki/Coppertone_(sunscreen)

https://en.wikipedia.org/wiki/Sunscreen

https://skincare.lovetoknow.com/Clearasil

http://www.pbs.org/wnet/need-to-know/health/a-brief-history-of-the-birth-control-pill/480/

https://www.history.com/this-day-in-history/fda-approves-the-pill

https://www.theatlantic.com/health/archive/2014/01/the-death-of-the-cool-feminist-smoker/283273/

https://en.wikipedia.org/wiki/Virginia_Slims

https://en.wikipedia.org/wiki/Virginia_Slims_Circuit

https://en.wikipedia.org/wiki/1983_Virginia_Slims_Hall_of_Fame_Classic

 Clearasil

Who can forget acne (colloquially known as pimples) – the bane of our teenage existence? Boomer adolescents were the primary target audience when it came to acne medication brand marketing. In 1950, acne treatments already existed but they were not widely used; a large market remained untapped. Ivan Combe, a businessman, teamed up with Kedzie Teller, a chemist, to create an acne-fighting cream the color of flesh. They named it Clearasil. Retailers, however, were not receptive to the brand until Combe, an aggressive marketer, offered them tubes of the product for free. Only then did retailers put Clearasil on their shelves, and lo and behold, it quickly gained popularity with Boomers. After a while, Clearasil achieved such success that it became one of only two brands to sponsor Dick Clark's "American Bandstand" (the other brand was Cheerios). Combe sold Clearasil to Vick Chemical in 1960. Today, the brand is owned by Reckitt Benckiser and Clearasil is marketed internationally.

Photo credit: Clearasil product photo

 Coppertone

Invented by pharmacist Benjamin Green in 1944, Coppertone was a lotion originally intended to protect American soldiers in World War II from the sun. Coppertone achieved national recognition through its "Coppertone girl" advertising campaign that launched in the 50s. Illustrated by Joyce Ballantyne Brand using her daughter Cheri as the model, the Coppertone girl famously had her bathing suit pulled down by a puppy, revealing a pale bottom. The coy slogan, "Don't be a paleface!" served to enhance the image's popularity, which appeared in ads and on billboards across the nation. In the 60s, four-year old Jodie Foster appeared in a television commercial as the Coppertone girl. The early version of Coppertone provided minimal sunscreen protection; the sun protection factor ("SPF") calculations for sunscreens were not adopted in the United States until 1978. Coppertone continues to be a leading sunscreen brand today.

Photo credit: Miamism on VisualHunt.com. Licensed under the Creative Commons Attribution 2.0 Generic license.

The Pill

The birth control pill, widely known as "The Pill," was brought to market just in time for the sexual revolution started by the Boomers. The development of the pill took place throughout the 50s. Research was commissioned by the birth control advocate, Margaret Sanger, and funded by the wealthy women's rights activist Katherine McCormick. Sanger opened the country's first birth control clinic in 1916 and started an organization called the American Birth Control League, the forerunner of Planned Parenthood. Human trials of the birth control pill were conducted by biochemist Gregory Pincus and gynecologist John Rock in 1954. Then in 1960, the Food and Drug Administration approved the birth control pill for contraceptive use. Enovid was the brand name of the first hormonal birth control pill, which had to be taken daily and was prescribed only for married women when first introduced. By 1963, over two million women were taking the pill, which has become a common form of birth control today.

Photo credit: Bruce Blaus. Licensed under the Creative Commons Attribution 4.0 International license.

 Virginia Slims

Virginia Slims was the first cigarette brand to target women smokers when it was introduced in 1968. The Philip Morris Company's Virginia Slims brand, a companion to the Benson & Hedges brand, was packaged and advertised as cigarettes just for females. The cigarettes were long and narrow, designed to look elegant between a woman's fingers. The tone of the ad copy and the advertising tagline created a sensation: "You've come a long way, baby." Used extensively to advertise Virginia Slims for close to thirty years, this slogan is one of the most notable in advertising history. To enhance its brand image, Virginia Slims cleverly associated itself with women's tennis, forming the Virginia Slims Circuit in 1970, made up of nine professional female tennis players. One of the players, Billie Jean King, went on to beat Bobby Riggs in the 1973 "Battle of the Sexes" tennis match. Other cigarette brands, such as Eve, tried to appeal to women, but none were as successful as Virginia Slims, which is still being sold today.

Photo credit: Joe Haupt on Flickr.com. Licensed under the Creative Commons Attribution ShareAlike 2.0 Generic license.

On the Road Again

In the 50s and 60s, Americans were in love with automobiles. During those decades, the automobile industry literally fueled the American economy. The largest industrial segment ever created, the American automobile industry in the 50s dwarfed all of the world's other automakers combined.

Many conditions converged to make the 50s the high point of the American auto industry. The end of World War II spurred a renewed interest in national economic development, automobile technology was improving significantly, and Americans were ready to invest in family cars. Just as important, President Eisenhower endorsed the Interstate Highway System, which was authorized in 1956. Serviceable roads eventually stretched from coast to coast.

The automobile industry responded by feverishly producing countless car brands in the 50s and 60s. Some car brands were so strong they overshadowed the name of the manufacturer

(Corvette and Mustang, for example). Previously independent carmakers either disappeared or were swallowed up by a group of manufacturers known as the "Big Three" – Chrysler, Ford, and General Motors. During the 50s and 60s, a fourth automaker, AMC, created by a merger of Nash and Hudson, was also prominent. (Maybe you remember AMC's ugly "Gremlin.")

Family car models were the core of auto production, but the Boomer era also saw the rapid rise of "muscle" cars – cars prized for their performance, power, and speed. Car brands became so loved by the Boomer generation that they were immortalized in songs such as "Fun, Fun, Fun," "GTO," "Hey Little Cobra," and "Little Deuce Coupe." Popular books paying homage to the automobile and road travel included Jack Kerouac's "On the Road" (1957) and John Steinbeck's "Travels with Charley" (1962). Movies ("Bullitt" starring Steve McQueen) and television shows ("Route 66," and "Car 54, Where are You?") also celebrated our car culture.

"Road trip" quickly entered the American vernacular. Family vacation time was likely to revolve around cars. The car culture caught fire, creating a burgeoning market for movie drive-ins, fast food restaurants, roadside motels, shopping malls and car washes. In 1951, the world's first drive-thru wedding chapel opened in Las Vegas. Even now, automobiles are still "sacred cars" to Americans.

Why We Loved Car Brands

There was a whole country to explore and, during our childhood, the car was the transportation method of choice.

Television promoted national travel and automakers glamorized road trips in their advertising ("See the USA in your Chevrolet"). Automobile ads were everywhere we looked, and car dealerships were prominent in most towns. The family car may have been a sedan or a station wagon. In the early 50s, maybe your family was lucky enough to own one of the last "woodies" ever made – station wagons with real wood siding.

Summers always presented a challenge for parents when their children were out of school. Boomer kids whose families could afford it went to camps, but for two glorious weeks during summer vacation, most families packed up the car for a road trip. Maybe you remember fighting with your siblings on those lengthy journeys. There was nothing better than hanging your bare feet out the car window, discovering exotic places, and stopping at a Howard Johnson's restaurant for lunch or ice cream.

Automobile travel back then was adventurous for families. No seat belts, no car seats, and often no air conditioning. No GPS to get you where you were going (thank goodness for AAA "Triptik") and no ATMs along the way. Maybe your dad was one of the few fortunate individuals to have a Diner's Club credit card or he'd buy American Express traveler's checks in advance, but that was unlikely.

Kids, especially boys, got hooked on car brands. As we matured, lots of us lusted after Corvettes, GTOs and Mustangs. We glorified the tough guys who dared to drag race. Learning to drive was a significant rite of passage for all of us, closely aligned with "growing up." Once we learned to drive, we learned a lot of other things: How to cruise the streets on week-ends, how to impress our friends, how to use those drive-in movie speakers, and how to find secluded spots to make out in the back seat. A car may have even been the all-hallowed location where some of us lost our virginity. Ah, the memories!

During our rebellious years, cars represented an escape route from our families and our home towns. The Volkswagen brand, in particular, became associated with the counter-culture movement: Hippies camped out in VW Microbuses and the VW "Bug" was symbolic of a less materialistic, more mobile and free generation.

Some of the popular Boomer era car brands are listed below. Which ones do *you* remember?

Buick Roadmaster * Cadillac Fleetwood * Chevy Camaro * Chevy Corvette * Corvette Sting Ray * Dodge Charger * Ford Mustang * Ford Thunderbird * Oldsmobile 88 * Plymouth Road Runner * Pontiac Firebird * Pontiac GTO * Rambler American * Volkswagen Bus * Volkswagen "Bug"

The following trademarks and registered trademarks are the property of their respective holders: AMC, Buick Roadmaster, Bullitt, Cadillac, Camaro, Charger, Chevron, Chevy, Chevrolet, Chrysler, Cobra, Corvette, Dodge, Firebird, Fleetwood, Ford, General Motors, GM, Goldfinger, GTO, Hudson, Indianapolis 500, James Bond, Mustang, Nash, Oldsmobile, Oldsmobile 88, Plymouth, Pontiac, Rambler American, Sting Ray, Texaco, Thunderbird, Volkswagen, VW

Sources

https://en.wikipedia.org/wiki/Automotive_industry_in_the_United_States

https://en.wikipedia.org/wiki/American_automobile_industry_in_the_1950s

https://en.wikipedia.org/wiki/1950s_American_automobile_culture

https://www.historicvehicle.org/how-the-automobile-shaped-america-culture/

http://wishyouwerehere.us/article/worlds-first-drive-thru-wedding-chapel

https://www.gentlemansgazette.com/muscle-cars-explained-history/

https://www.edmunds.com/chevrolet/corvette/history.html

https://www.caranddriver.com/news/chevrolet-corvette-timeline-milestones-and-more-from-c1-through-c7

https://en.wikipedia.org/wiki/Chevrolet_Corvette

https://en.wikipedia.org/wiki/Ford_Mustang

https://www.cjponyparts.com/resources/ford-mustang-history

https://en.wikipedia.org/wiki/Texaco

https://en.wikipedia.org/wiki/Texaco_Star_Theatre

Corvette

The "Vette," as the Corvette is lovingly known to its fans, was an audacious move on the part of General Motors – it was the company's first sports car. Conceived by a GM designer in the early 50s, the Corvette was a convertible intended to be only a show car. The company's chief engineer was so enthusiastic about the Corvette, though, that he had the prototype car made ready for production. Good thing he did. When the Corvette, named for a small warship, debuted, it drew the interest of thousands of potential buyers. GM rushed the car into production, and the first one came off the line in mid-1953, just six months after its unveiling. By 1956, the high-performance Vette established its reputation as a race car. The brand was burnished by the 1963 introduction of the Corvette Sting Ray, which helped the Corvette line top 20,000 units sold for the first time. The 1983 smash hit by Prince, "Little Red Corvette," further hyped the brand name. By 2011, seven Corvette models were available, and today, the Vette is considered one of the most celebrated and esteemed of American sports cars.

Photo credit: Pixabay.com

Mustang

In 1964, more than a decade after the Chevy Corvette was born, the Ford Mustang came galloping along. It was an immediate success: Ford projected 100,000 Mustangs would be sold each year, but in the first twelve months, the company sold over 400,000 of them. Unlike a true "muscle car," the Mustang is credited with being the first "pony car," which came to mean a sporty, stylish performance car that was small and affordable. Right from the start, the new Ford brand had a certain cachet. The Mustang was the pace car for the Indianapolis 500 in 1964; that same year, it was featured in the James Bond movie, "Goldfinger." It wasn't long before racing versions of the car, such as the GT 350 (1965) and the GT 500 (1967), were introduced. In the 1968 movie "Bullitt," Steve McQueen drove a Mustang GT 390. "Bullitt" later became the name of a Mustang GT package and a Mustang Bullitt nameplate. It wasn't until the 70s that the famed Mustang Cobra line was introduced. The Mustang was rumored to be on the chopping block by Ford in the 2000s, but a public outcry kept the brand alive and kicking.

Photo credit: Pixabay.com

Texaco

Texaco is the brand of gasoline most Boomer kids recognized for two reasons: First, early on Texaco was the biggest selling gasoline brand, and the only oil company to sell gasoline in all fifty states and Canada under one brand name. Second, Texaco sponsored one of the first popular television variety shows, "Texaco Star Theater." Texaco shortened its name from the Texas Fuel Company during the 50s and used a star, representative of Texas, in its logo. The advertising jingle, "You can trust your car to the man who wears the star," was recognized wide and far. Texaco became a household brand name because of its association with "Texaco Star Theater," a comedy-variety show, first on radio (1939 – 1949) and then on television (1948 – 1953). The TV show featured comedian Milton Berle, also affectionately known as "Uncle Miltie," who became a television icon. Buick took over sponsorship of the show in 1953, but in 1955, Texaco became the sole sponsor of the "Huntley-Brinkley Report," so the Texaco brand name remained prominent on television. Now owned by Chevron Corporation, the Texaco brand can still be seen adorning some gas stations.

Photo credit: Pixabay.com

Orange You Hungry?

One of America's most prominent Boomer era brands wasn't a product – it was a restaurant. The unique orange roof of a Howard Johnson's restaurant was a kind of beacon of safety for Boomer kids and their families when they traveled the roads of America in the 50s and 60s. Families could depend on the chain's consistency, affordability, food quality, and friendliness of the service, wherever a Howard Johnson's was located.

There really was a Howard Johnson. A New Englander, Johnson opened an ice cream shop not far from Boston, in Quincy, Massachusetts in 1925, crafting his own ice cream with a high butterfat content and natural ingredients. The ice cream was a hit with customers, so much so that he began to sell it at stands and other locations. He then expanded the ice cream shop into a restaurant.

The Great Depression put a damper on Johnson's ambition to open more restaurants, but he wasn't deterred. Instead of investing a lot of his own money, Johnson conceived of a novel idea: Restaurant franchising. In return for franchise fees, he would provide the name, supply the food, and create a system for others to operate Howard Johnson restaurants. It was Johnson who first thought of preparing food in a central location and shipping it to restaurants, where it was cooked and served with remarkable consistency from one restaurant to another. Fast food restaurants would later adopt his idea. Johnson didn't skimp on quality, either. He hired top chefs to oversee food production and provided Dior-designed uniforms for the trained waitresses.

By the late 1930s, the East Coast from Massachusetts to Florida was dotted with more than 100 Howard Johnson's restaurants, including the nation's first turnpike restaurant on the Pennsylvania Turnpike. A key part of the chain's expansion strategy was to locate along highways and near transportation centers, like railroad depots. In fact, Johnson's original restaurant design was modeled after a railroad station in Quincy, Massachusetts. Howard Johnson's restaurants were so successful that by 1965, the chain's sales surpassed McDonald's, Burger King, and Kentucky Fried Chicken *combined*. At its height, Howard Johnson's restaurants numbered over 1,000.

To capitalize on America's love affair with car road trips, Howard Johnson Motor Lodges were created by the company beginning in 1954. Some of them were attached to Howard Johnson's restaurants. More than 500 Howard Johnson Motor Lodges existed by the 70s.

Everyone, especially kids, recognized the Howard Johnson brand name, sometimes referring to it as "HoJo." Kids were also very familiar with the restaurant logo – Simple Simon and the Pieman. No one could miss the renowned orange roof and teal spire, topped by a weathervane, or the large neon sign at the front entrance.

By the 70s, however, the restaurant chain was in decline. As of the publication of *Boomer Brands*, there is one remaining Howard Johnson's restaurant in Lake George, New York. Wyndham Hotels bought the rights to the Howard Johnson name and operates modern-day Howard Johnson hotels featuring retro décor.

Why We Loved Howard Johnson

For most of us, going to a Howard Johnson's restaurant with our parents was a memorable, fun, and delicious experience. Howard Johnson's was a colorful, happy place that catered to kids, right down to crayons, coloring pages and a kid's menu.

At Howard Johnson's, you may have had your first introduction to corn "toastees," or "tender-sweet" fried clam strips with tartare sauce. It was Howard Johnson who came up with the idea of removing the bellies from fried clams to make them kid-friendly; they became very popular with adults, too. And nothing could beat the Howard Johnson's "frankfort," gently split down the middle, grilled in butter and served in the restaurant's signature toasted white bread bun.

But the best reason of all to love Howard Johnson's had to be the ice cream. In the 50s, most restaurants and even ice cream shops were still serving up the standard three flavors: chocolate, vanilla, and strawberry. Howard Johnson changed all that by offering 28 flavors. He reportedly said, "I thought I had every flavor in the world. That '28' became my trademark." For old time's sake, here is a list of all 28 flavors of Howard Johnson's ice cream, as listed on the nostalgic website, HoJoLand.com: Banana, Black Raspberry, Burgundy Cherry, Butter Pecan, Buttercrunch, Butterscotch, Caramel Fudge, Chocolate, Chocolate Chip, Coconut, Coffee, Frozen Pudding, Fruit Salad, Fudge Ripple, Lemon Stick, Macaroon, Maple Walnut, Mocha Chip, Orange-Pineapple, Peach, Peanut Brittle, Pecan Brittle, Peppermint Stick, Pineapple, Pistachio, Strawberry, Strawberry Ripple, Vanilla.

Long before we discovered McDonald's "Happy Meals," Howard Johnson was our go-to place for comfort food.

The following trademarks and registered trademarks are the property of their respective holders: 28, Bumbershoot's, Chatt's, Deli Baker Ice Cream Maker, Ground Round, Happy Meal, HoJo, HoJoLand, Howard Johnson, Howard Johnson's, McDonald's, Paddywacks, Pickle Lily's, Red Coach Grill, Wyndham Hotels

Sources

http://www.hojoland.com/history.html

https://en.wikipedia.org/wiki/Howard_Johnson%27s

http://www.slamtrak.com/hojo2003/

HoJo Brands

In addition to Howard Johnson's restaurants and Howard Johnson Motor Lodges, the company spawned additional places and products that leveraged the Howard Johnson brand name and, in many cases, the orange-and-teal color scheme. Other Howard Johnson-branded restaurants included Howard Johnson's Ice Cream Shop, HoJo's Whistle Stop Fast Food Restaurant, and HoJo Junction Fast Food Restaurant. The Howard Johnson brand name appeared on turnpike vending centers. There were HoJo Campgrounds. At the height of its popularity, Howard Johnson introduced a line of frozen foods so consumers could satisfy their HoJo craving at home. (Orange Toastees were my personal favorite; my daughter loved them too.) As the company expanded, it also created other restaurant brands, most of which no longer exist: Bumbershoot's, Chatt's, Deli Baker Ice Cream Maker, Ground Round, Paddywacks, Pickle Lily's, and Red Coach Grill. There has been an interest in relaunching the Howard Johnson brand name with either restaurants or food products, but that hasn't happened yet.

Photo credit: Boston Public Library on VisualHunt.com. Licensed under the Creative Commons Attribution 2.0 Generic license.

Burgers Galore
and More

Howard Johnson's may have been the ultimate roadside restaurant brand during the Boomer era, but it isn't credited with beginning the American fast food restaurant craze. That distinction goes to burger restaurants. The brand name most often associated with fast food burgers is McDonald's, but here's a fun fact: McDonald's was *not* the first fast food establishment to serve up burgers. That distinction goes to a chain called White Castle.

Opened in 1921 in Wichita, Kansas by Billy Ingram, White Castle started much like other burger brands, with one small restaurant. That first store actually did look like a diminutive "white castle," and others soon followed. The restaurant made little five-cent square burgers called "Sliders" that were so popular they were sold by the sack. Presto, the fast food burger chain was born. Also in 1921, a new idea called the "drive-in" was conceived by a restaurant chain in Texas, the Pig Stand. Customers would drive up to the Pig Stand and "carhops" would serve food by bringing it on trays that attached to car windows. Then in 1948, a California burger restaurant, In-N-Out, probably developed the very first drive-thru operation: Customers could place an order, drive up to a window, and get their food without needing to leave their cars. White Castle, the Pig Stand, and In-N-Out would soon be eclipsed by other burger chains, drive-ins and drive-thrus whose brand names would become far better known.

One of them was McDonald's, which began making burgers in 1948 and started its franchise operation in 1954. By 1958, the chain had sold 100 million burgers. That success spawned a slew of fast food burger competitors, including Jack in the Box (1950), Insta-Burger King, later shortened to Burger King (1953), Burger Chef (1954), Hardee's (1960), and Wendy's (1969).

Since there's more to life than burgers, other fast food operators appropriated the franchise concept and created such famous Boomer era chains as Dunkin' Donuts (1950), Taco Bell (1954), Kentucky Fried Chicken (1955), Pizza Hut (1958), Sonic (1959), Little Caesar's (1962), Arby's (1964), Domino's (1965), Chick-fil-A (1967), and Subway (1968). It's remarkable to think these chains all grew up when we did. Just as amazing is that these fast food brand names still exist, and each brand continues to have its own position in the industry.

The real success of fast food restaurants, of course, remains a winning combination of value and convenience. The longevity of fast food restaurants in America and worldwide cannot be challenged, but they have come under fire in recent years for the questionable health benefits of the food they serve.

Why We Loved Burger and Fast Food Brands

The hamburger's origin stretches back thousands of years. As for the American burger, though, that tasty patty of ground beef is thought to have originated as a "Hamburg steak," brought to this country by European immigrants in the mid- to late-1800s. As mentioned earlier, while White Castle legitimized the burger as early as the 1920s, burger hysteria reached its height during the Boomer era.

For a lot of us during our childhood, we didn't really care about how the hamburger got its start, we just wanted to eat more of them. There was nothing better than a burger with ketchup on a bun – accompanied by fries, of course. We couldn't get enough of burgers, whether they were served to us by mom at home, at the local soda shop, or at our favorite fast food place. The perfect melding of fast food and car culture was a drive-in that served burgers and fries.

If you were like other Boomer kids, you had your favorite fast food burger brand. At the risk of being exclusionary, it was likely to be either McDonald's or Burger King. To this day, these burger behemoths continue to battle it out in an effort to win new burger fans and retain old ones. It's a well-known marketing strategy for one burger chain to open a location right near another burger chain; strangely, both brands seem to benefit.

Restaurant franchising has worked well beyond the burger chains. Eventually, as our tastes broadened to fried chicken, pizza, tacos and the like, the fast food industry followed along, only too happy to oblige our desires. The cuisine may have varied but the overarching goal of value combined with convenience was still the same. Unfortunately, all of the nutritionally bankrupt wonders sold at these establishments in the early years were loaded with enough fat and salt to keep us kids craving more, more, more. And of course, the food was typically served with sugary sweet soft drinks, or rich, sugar-laden shakes. That hasn't changed much today. To some extent, however, fast food chains are trying to upgrade their menus by adding healthier food choices.

Admit it: You may have cringed when your own children clamored for fast food burgers (including the toys that accompanied the kids' meals) – but you probably caved in and visited the "Golden Arches" or the "King" when they were young 'uns. After all, it's hard to deny your child the delight of a brand you yourself grew up with.

Some of the popular Boomer era burger brands and other fast food restaurant brands are listed below. Which ones were *your* favorites?

Arby's * Burger Chef * Burger King * Chick-fil-A * Domino's * Dunkin' Donuts * Hardee's * In-N-Out * Jack in the Box * Kentucky Fried Chicken * Little Caesar's * McDonald's * Pizza Hut * Sonic * Subway * Taco Bell * Wendy's * White Castle * White Tower

The following trademarks and registered trademarks are the property of their respective holders: Arby's, Burger Chef, Burger King, Chick-fil-A, Coca-Cola, Coke, Domino's, Dunkin' Donuts, Hardees, In-N-Out, Jack in the Box, Kentucky Fried Chicken, KFC, Little Caesar's, McDonald's, Multimixer, Pizza Hut, Sonic, Subway, Taco Bell, Wendy's, White Castle, White Tower

Sources

https://www.whitecastle.com/about/company/our-story

https://www.metv.com/lists/8-fast-food-chains-you-wish-you-could-eat-at-again

https://www.usatoday.com/story/travel/destinations/2014/05/31/fast-food-chains-origins/9729901/

https://www.accupos.com/pos-articles/history-of-fast-food-in-america/

https://livinghistoryfarm.org/farminginthe50s/farm-life/fast-foods/

https://www.history.com/news/fries-with-that-a-brief-history-of-drive-thru-dining

https://www.thevintagenews.com/2017/06/15/the-birth-of-the-fast-food-restaurant-photos-the-origins-of-our-most-popular-chains/

https://whatscookingamerica.net/History/HamburgerHistory.htm

https://www.kfc.com/about

https://www.biography.com/people/colonel-harland-sanders-12353545

https://en.wikipedia.org/wiki/History_of_KFC

https://www.nytimes.com/2014/05/16/business/coke-and-mcdonalds-working-hand-in-hand-since-1955.html

http://www.historyvshollywood.com/reelfaces/founder/

https://www.mcdonalds.com/us/en-us/about-us/our-history.html

http://blog.pizzahut.com/our-story/

Kentucky Fried Chicken

Colonel Sanders, the originator of Kentucky Fried Chicken, is as iconic as the restaurant chain itself. At the age of 40, Harland David Sanders started serving country food to travelers. He soon began to make and sell fried chicken. His successful business came to the attention of Kentucky Governor Ruby Laffoon who, in 1935, awarded Sanders the honorary title of "Kentucky Colonel." By 1940, Colonel Sanders had created his "original recipe" of eleven spices and herbs and was frying chicken in a specially modified pressure fryer. At age 62, the Colonel began traveling around the country, convincing restaurants to use his recipe and pay him a nickel for every chicken sold. The name "Kentucky Fried Chicken" was created by restaurant owner Pete Harman in Salt Lake City, Utah. Harman is said to have also come up with the slogan, "It's finger lickin' good." In a few years, Sanders had signed up several franchisees, one of whom was Dave Thomas, who later started Wendy's. Kentucky Fried Chicken, or KFC, now has over 21,000 outlets in 130 countries and territories – the world's largest chicken restaurant chain.

Photo credit: Pixabay.com

McDonald's

Brothers Mac and Dick McDonald started serving barbecue in 1940 but switched to burgers in 1948. Mixer salesman Ray Kroc visited their busy San Bernardino, California location in 1954 and he was so impressed that he began working for the two brothers. In 1955, Kroc founded the McDonald's System, Inc., the forerunner of McDonald's Corporation. (His story is dramatized in "The Founder," a 2017 movie starring Michael Keaton as Kroc). Kroc franchised the concept. His approach to the business was to create a system that allowed franchisees and suppliers to work for themselves in partnership with McDonald's. Creative franchisees invented many of the restaurant's signature menu items, including the Big Mac and Egg McMuffin. One supplier, Coca-Cola, began a relationship with Kroc in 1955 that remains to this day – so important that the soft drink company has a division devoted just to McDonald's. The "Golden Arches" symbolize one of the world's most recognized brands, with some 36,000 locations in 101 countries.

Photo credit: Pixabay.com

Pizza Hut

In 1958, two brothers named Dan and Frank Carney started their own pizza restaurant in a little hut in Wichita Kansas. Logically, they named the place Pizza Hut. (There was another reason for the name: The sign they used only had room for eight letters!) The Carney brothers gave away free pizza in an effort to get their first customers. In six months, they opened another Pizza Hut, and by the end of their first year, they had six restaurants. In 1969, Pizza Hut's iconic red roof was introduced, and by 1971, Pizza Hut had become the number one pizza restaurant chain in the world, both in sales and number of restaurants. Little Caesar's and Domino's were early competitors, forcing Pizza Hut to eventually add delivery to its restaurant operation. Today owned by Yum! Brands (also the owner of KFC and Taco Bell), Pizza Hut has been aggressively creative in keeping its brand in the public eye. In 2016, for example, the chain set a world record, making a pizza delivery to Mt. Kilimanjaro to celebrate opening in its 100th country.

Photo credit: DNO1967b on VisualHunt.com. Licensed under the Creative Commons Attribution 2.0 Generic license.

Reelin' and Rockin'

All generations have their music, but for many Boomers, music defined our generation. Boomer kids seemed to be right in the middle of a sea change in music, and they would help fuel it with their love of "rock 'n' roll."

The roots of rock 'n' roll go back to rhythm and blues (R&B), a genre dominated by African-Americans. Some say white artists appropriated R&B songs and added their own sound to make them into rock 'n' roll songs. In fact, rock 'n' roll songwriters of the 50s were mostly white and predominantly Jewish. Others say rock 'n' roll merged many musical influences – R&B, doo-wop, boogie, jazz, gospel, and even country. Most rock historians generally agree that rock 'n' roll was named in the early 50s by an Ohio disc jockey, Alan Freed. He coined the term to represent a new kind of upbeat music that had broad appeal across African-American and white teens.

However it got its start, rock 'n' roll was a brand of music that was uniquely ours. Some of its popularity was surely because it was viewed as "rebel music" by our elders. Early on, technology helped rock 'n' roll grow exponentially: The 50s saw the introduction of the solid body electric guitar (the heart of rock groups), the 45 RPM record (an inexpensive way for us to own rock songs), and the transistor radio (providing us with a portable listening experience), all of which contributed to rock's rapid rise. And then, of course, there was television. The wildly popular "American Bandstand" and appearances by rock stars on such family programs as "The Ed Sullivan Show" helped popularize rock 'n' roll in a way no other medium could.

When rock met the revolutionary times of the 60s and 70s, it morphed into folk rock, protest rock, British rock, acid or psychedelic rock, and eventually heavy metal rock and punk rock. But let's not get ahead of ourselves... we'll stay firmly rooted in our childhood memories.

Record labels were brands. The Motown record label was such a super-brand that it became recognized for "the Motown sound." But generally, labels were not nearly as significant as musical artists. What you may not have considered is that the rock 'n' roll artists we listened to and dearly loved were themselves personal brands. Elvis (no surname required) was most definitely a brand. So was Bob Dylan. So were The Temptations, The Beach Boys, and The Beatles.

Why We Loved Rock 'n' Roll Brands

Many of our childhood experiences were linked to music, often to a particular rock 'n' roll song. As adolescents, individual songs permeated our consciousness and defined important moments in our lives. A specific song could be associated with something good (a first kiss), something bad (a breakup with a girl or boy), something freeing (learning to drive), something strange (a drug trip), or even something traumatic (being drafted). We knew the lyrics to our favorite songs, sang to them, and danced to them. We sat glued to the television as Dick Clark asked kids to rate songs on his TV show.

Songs also reflected the times. They gave voice to protest, peace, and hope. There were songs we sang to resist the war, fight for civil rights, and march for equality. Sometimes songs made us laugh, other times they made us cry. Sometimes they had obvious messages and sometimes their meanings were hidden. (Despite rumors surrounding several songs by The Beatles, for instance, we were relieved to find out that Paul was not dead after all.)

We not only had favorite songs, we had favorite performing artists. We bought their records, attended their concerts, and joined their fan clubs. Some of us may have even been their groupies. Boys may have tried to emulate rock bands by covering their songs on their own instruments. (I was a drummer in a short-lived band that played 60s hits.) Girls may have screamed with delight when Elvis appeared on television. And nothing compared to the wild, unadulterated hysteria we felt when we saw The Beatles live and in person at Shea Stadium in New York City (1965). Or the unworldly experience of listening to the likes of Joan Baez, Jimi Hendrix, and The Who while being stoned with hundreds of thousands of hippies at Woodstock (1969).

Some popular Boomer era rock 'n' roll brands are listed below. Which ones were *your* favorites?

Music Television Shows
American Bandstand * Hullabaloo * Shindig * Soul Train

Record Labels (50s and 60s)
Atlantic * Capitol * Chess * Columbia * Decca * Elektra * Epic * Mercury * Motown * Stax * Sun * RCA * Reprise

Performing Artists – Individuals (50s and 60s)
Paul Anka * Joan Baez * Chuck Berry * James Brown * Sam Cooke * Bobby Darin * Neil Diamond * Fats Domino * Bob Dylan * Connie Francis * Aretha Franklin * Marvin Gaye * Buddy Holly * Janis Joplin * Jerry Lee Lewis * Johnny Mathis * Wilson Pickett * Elvis Presley * Otis Redding * Johnny Rivers * Neil Sedaka * Pete Seeger * Dionne Warwick * Stevie Wonder

Performing Artists – Groups (50s and 60s)
The Beach Boys * The Beatles * The Byrds * The Coasters * Cream * Creedence Clearwater Revival * Crosby Stills Nash and Young * The Dave Clark Five * Dion and the Belmonts * The Doors * The Drifters * The Everly Brothers * The Four Seasons * The Four Tops * Grateful Dead * Jan and Dean * Jefferson Airplane * Jimi Hendrix Experience * The Kinks * Gladys Knight and the Pips * Lovin' Spoonful * Martha and the Vandellas * The Monkees * Peter, Paul and Mary * The Platters * The Rascals * Smokey Robinson and the Miracles * The Rolling Stones * The Shirelles * Simon & Garfunkel * The Supremes * The Temptations * The Who

Sources

https://www.newyorker.com/magazine/2015/11/16/the-elvic-oracle

http://www.rockmusictimeline.com/

https://en.wikipedia.org/wiki/Rock_and_roll

http://www.waybackattack.com/top100-musicartists.html

http://www.the60sofficialsite.com/The_Top_100_Recording_Artists_of_the_50s_and_60s_Era.html

https://www.history.com/this-day-in-history/american-bandstand-goes-national

https://en.wikipedia.org/wiki/American_Bandstand

https://parade.com/592309/jerylbrunner/8-surprising-facts-about-the-legendary-dance-show-american-bandstand/

https://en.wikipedia.org/wiki/The_Monkees

https://people.com/music/micky-dolenz-on-the-monkees-50th-anniversary-album-and-tour/

https://www.monkees.com/

https://en.wikipedia.org/wiki/Motown

https://www.motownmuseum.org/story/motown/

http://content.time.com/time/arts/article/0,8599,1870975,00.html

American Bandstand

Rock 'n' roll first emerged in 1952, so that's when a local Philadelphia TV station aired "Bandstand," a music show aimed at teens. It was hosted by a radio DJ, Bob Horn. When Dick Clark took over in 1956, the show remained local – until he lobbied ABC to put it on national television. "American Bandstand" aired in 1957. Clark insisted that the teens who appeared on the show – regular kids, not actors – all dress neatly and be well-behaved. The "Rate-a-Record" feature, in which two members of the audience gave their opinions of two records, was especially popular. Many top performers appeared live on the show, but they all lip synced (except Jerry Lee Lewis), because Clark wanted the songs to sound exactly like the recorded versions. "American Bandstand" aired live at 3:30 PM, five days a week, until 1963, when it became a taped, weekly program. Dick Clark remained the host for twenty-four years. Anniversary specials aired right up until the 50th Anniversary Edition of "American Bandstand," hosted by Dick Clark in 2002.

The Monkees

The Monkees were more of a *brand* than a *band*, at least initially. Two producers, Bob Rafelson and Bert Schneider, found inspiration in the fact that The Beatles were able to leverage their musical success into making a movie called "A Hard Day's Night." Why not build a television series around an American band, the producers thought? They sold the idea to Screen Gems and "The Monkees" began a two-year run on television in 1966. Initially, Rafelson and Schneider wanted to use a real band, the Lovin' Spoonful, but a recording contract conflicted with their plans, so instead, they recruited actors. The twist to the show – which ended up being controversial – was that the actors were never supposed to play "real" music. As a result, professional musicians performed the actual music, which was written by top songwriters of the day. The media lampooned the concept, fans were appalled, and the actors (Micky Dolenz, Davy Jones, Michael Nesmith, and Peter Tork) rebelled. They then began playing concerts and recording albums by themselves, and the television brand turned into a real band after all. The TV show began in 1966 and ended its run in 1968, but The

Monkees band achieved legitimate musical success through 1971, selling more than 75 million records worldwide. There have been numerous reunion tours since then and even releases of new albums. After the death of Jones in 2012, Dolenz and Tork teamed up for more tours and were occasionally joined by Nesmith.

Photo credit: Pixabay.com

Motown

Motown was a record label brand that became symbolic of a vibrant, contemporary style of African-American music. It enjoyed wide popularity and cut across racial barriers during the turbulent 60s. Founded in 1959 by former boxer-autoworker Berry Gordy Jr., the record label was named "Motown" by Gordy to celebrate his hometown of Detroit, the Motor City. Gordy is credited with instituting a factory-like discipline in music production, assembling a cadre of African-American artists, both individual performers and groups, and making music so unique it was referred to as "the Motown Sound." From the very start, Berry adorned his small building on West Grand Boulevard with the sign "Hitsville U.S.A." At the time, it was wishful thinking, but Gordy made it a reality with his drive, charisma, and business acumen, combined with the raw talent of such performers as The Four Tops, Martha and the Vandellas, Marvin Gaye, The Jackson Five, Gladys Knight and the Pips, The Supremes, Smokey Robinson and the Miracles, The Temptations, and Stevie Wonder. In 1968, Motown artists dominated the *Billboard Hot 100* with five out of the top ten hits. Motown became both the most successful African-American-owned record label and the most successful independent record company in history. The early 70s saw the relocation of Motown to Los Angeles, as the company expanded into television and film production. Today, Motown is owned by Universal Music Group, and the Motown Sound remains popular with Boomers as well as younger generations who have discovered a genre of music that remains timeless.

Photo credit: Ken Lund on VisualHunt.com. Licensed under the Creative Commons Attribution ShareAlike 2.0 Generic license.

Politics and Protest

No one need remind Boomers of the turbulent 60s and 70s; older Boomers may have actively participated as protesters during those decades or gone off to war (willingly or unwillingly). These decades were troubled times at best and life-altering times at worst. The 60s and 70s even ended the lives of some of the people we knew and loved. So how can we relate something so serious to something so seemingly superficial as branding?

The answer is simple: When you broaden the definition of a brand, as I've done in this book, branding politics and protest becomes meaningful. Branding is a concrete way to identify notable people, places and things that have their own brand attributes and their own distinct significance. As a result, branding helps us define tangible things during a turbulent time.

The brands of politics and protest might be considered "consciousness brands." They include:

- *people brands*, such as John F. Kennedy, Martin Luther King, Malcolm X, Timothy Leary and Bobby Kennedy
- *place brands*, such as Berkeley, Kent State, Watergate, Woodstock and Vietnam
- *protest brands*, such as the peace sign, the slogan "Make Love, Not War," and the song "We Shall Overcome."

Thinking of each as a brand isolates, characterizes, and cements the place of every one of them in history. Each of these consciousness brands has a very personal meaning, defines a key moment, and evokes a powerful emotion.

Why We Connected with Consciousness Brands

Our collective consciousness, at least for Boomers entering young adulthood, probably began with the presidential campaign of a young, vibrant Massachusetts senator, John Fitzgerald Kennedy. JFK represented a new optimistic way forward for all of us.

The Kennedy-Nixon debate, the first to be televised, is an outstanding example of the extraordinary power of personal branding. The stark difference between the two candidates on television (a youthful, relaxed Kennedy and a sweating, uncomfortable Nixon) was a deciding factor in Kennedy's favor.

Boomer kids suddenly grew up when JFK was assassinated. Again, television played a key role as we watched Jackie Kennedy's unbelieving shock, Lyndon Johnson's swearing in, Jack Ruby's shooting of Lee Harvey Oswald, and Kennedy's children at his funeral. This marked the beginning of two of the stormiest decades in American history, including Vietnam, the first televised war.

Our consciousness was raised through civil rights, women's rights, and gay rights demonstrations, through anti-war protests, and through the unspeakable murders of such figures as Malcolm X, Martin Luther King, and Bobby Kennedy. Landmark civil rights legislation was passed. One president withdrew from running for a second term, and another president resigned from office. Protest signs were ubiquitous. Slogan buttons were wildly popular. Burning draft cards was in vogue. Smoking grass or hash and dropping acid were commonplace. The 1967 Summer of Love was legendary. A massive counterculture movement culminated in Woodstock. Is it any wonder some of us decided to drop out?

Here are some popular Boomer era consciousness "brands." Which of these were important to *you*?

People

Muhammad Ali * Spiro Agnew * Joan Baez * Daniel Berrigan * Julian Bond * Stokely Carmichael * Eldridge Cleaver * Archibald Cox * Angela Davis * Daniel Ellsberg * Jane Fonda * Betty Friedan * Tom Hayden * Abbie Hoffman * J. Edgar Hoover * Lyndon Johnson * Jackie Kennedy * John F. Kennedy * Robert Kennedy * Ken Kesey * Martin Luther King * Timothy Leary * Peter Max * Eugene McCarthy * Huey Newton * Richard Nixon * Lee Harvey Oswald * Jerry Rubin * Jack Ruby * Bobby Seale * Gloria Steinem * Andy Warhol * Malcolm X

Places

Berkeley * Birmingham * Greenwich Village * Haight Ashbury * Kent State * Monterey * Montgomery * Selma * Southeast Asia * Vietnam * Watergate * Woodstock

Protest
Black Panther Party * CORE * Moral Majority * NAACP * NOW * Peace Sign * SDS * SCLC * SNCC * Summer of Love * Vietnam Veterans Against the War * Yippies

Protest Songs
A Change is Gonna Come * Blowin' in the Wind * Eve of Destruction * Fortunate Son * For What It's Worth * Get Together * I Am Woman * Imagine * My Generation * Ohio * People Get Ready * Say It Loud, I'm Black and I'm Proud * Universal Soldier * We Are the World * We Shall Overcome * What's Goin' On

Slogans
America: Love It or Leave It * Ban the Bomb * Black is Beautiful * Black Power * Flower Power * Hell No, We Won't Go * If It Feels Good Do It * Make Love, Not War * Power to the People * Tune In Turn On Drop Out

The following trademarks and registered trademarks are the property of their respective holders: Black Panther Party, Black Panthers, CORE, Moral Majority, NAACP, NOW, Woodstock

Sources

https://en.m.wikipedia.org/wiki/Counterculture_of_the_1960s

http://adage.com/article/adage-encyclopedia/history-1960s/98702/

https://www.nytimes.com/2007/12/10/business/media/10adcol.html

https://uberbuttons.com/blog/10-iconic-buttons-from-the-civil-rights-era/

https://en.wikipedia.org/wiki/Black_Panther_Party

https://www.nytimes.com/2018/03/08/opinion/eugene-mccarthy-lyndon-johnson-vietnam.html

https://www.woodstock.com/

https://www.bethelwoodscenter.org/the-museum

Black Panther Party

The Black Panther Party was the brand most closely associated with the Black Power movement. Founded in 1966 by Huey Newton and Bobby Seale in Oakland, California, the party, also known as the Black Panthers, was a socialist-oriented movement organized in response to the murder of Malcolm X and, more generally, police brutality against African-Americans. While the Black Panthers Party was a militant organization, the group also worked to bring social programs to underserved communities, including free breakfast programs it served to school children and free health clinics it opened in African-American communities across the nation. Still, it was their violent clashes with police that made the Black Panthers a notorious brand of the time. In 1969, the Black Panther Party was labeled an "enemy of the United States government" by the FBI, under the leadership of J. Edgar Hoover. At its height, the Black Panther Party was said to have thousands of members, but internal strife, convictions, and continued harassment by local police and federal authorities spelled its demise in 1982.

Photo credit: Pixabay.com

Eugene McCarthy

U.S. Senator Eugene McCarthy (Minnesota) was the "person brand" known for first challenging President Lyndon Johnson for the Democratic nomination in 1968. Despite a lackluster personality, McCarthy enjoyed the enthusiastic support of young people, largely because he opposed the Vietnam war. At the time, state primaries were inconsequential. Still, a nasty occurrence in the war in early 1968 (the Tet Offensive) helped McCarthy obtain a remarkable 42 percent of the popular vote in the New Hampshire primary, while Johnson captured just 49 percent. McCarthy's strong showing convinced Senator Robert "Bobby" Kennedy, brother of JFK, to run for the nomination. Johnson withdrew; McCarthy and Kennedy battled bitterly while Hubert Humphrey became the "establishment" candidate. Bobby Kennedy was assassinated in June and McCarthy entered the Democratic Convention a popular favorite. Amidst furor and turmoil, however, he was defeated, and Humphrey became the Democratic presidential candidate.

Photo credit: Pixabay.com

Woodstock

Woodstock is such an iconic "place brand" that it continues to conjure up both positive and negative feelings about "sex, drugs and rock 'n' roll" decades later. It all started with four under-thirty entrepreneurs (John Roberts, Joel Rosenman, Michael Lang, and Artie Kornfeld) who got together to organize a music festival they pitched as "An Aquarian Exposition: 3 Days of Peace and Music." When the original location in upstate New York fell through, the dairy farm of Max Yasgur in Bethel, near the Catskill Mountains, became available as the spot for the August 1969 extravaganza. Woodstock featured an unprecedented line-up of super-star and counterculture musical performers that attracted over half a million young people, outnumbering the available 100,000 or so tickets. That meant most attendees were ultimately admitted at no charge. Roads were so clogged that the performers had to be airlifted in by helicopter. Despite driving rain, bad drug trips, and poor sanitary conditions, Woodstock became renowned as the singular event that defined the Boomer generation. Woodstock Ventures, the organization formed by the originators, continues to support events and projects in keeping with its founding principles. The Woodstock brand has spawned record albums, a film, videos, and books. The Museum at Bethel Woods was established to celebrate the 60s in general and Woodstock in particular. A 40th Anniversary concert commemorating Woodstock was held at the museum site in 2009.

Photo credit: Pixabay.com

Green Scene

The petri dish of the 60s was responsible for so many civil, social and political actions and revolutions that it is hard to keep track of them all. Most were touched on in "Politics and Protest," but one was intentionally omitted: Environmental activism. This deserves a chapter all its own, because the nascent environmental movement of the 60s gave birth to a whole class of green brands in subsequent decades.

While concern about the environment had been growing prior to the 60s, one Boomer era book was largely responsible for branding environmentalism. Scientist Rachel Carson's *Silent Spring*, first published as a series of three magazine articles in 1962, is widely credited with starting the environmental movement. The book began with a "fable for tomorrow," demonstrating how a pesticide called DDT was damaging life on earth.

Carson's documentation of the wide misuse of pesticides by humans and the harm it was causing was not embraced by everyone. She was lambasted by supporters of the chemical industry and had to defend her conclusions until her death in 1964. Still, the book achieved bestseller status and became an influential and timeless classic.

Another book contributed to environmentalism at about the same time. In 1964, *Unsafe at Any Speed* by attorney Ralph Nader was published. Nader's book was essentially an exposé of the American automobile industry, excoriating carmakers for their lack of attention to safety. The book largely concentrated on auto design flaws and safety dangers, but *Unsafe at Any Speed* included a chapter on the pollution caused by automobiles. Also a bestseller, Nader's book prompted safety legislation, most notably the passage of seat-belt laws.

These books were generally regarded as catalysts for the creation of the U.S. government's Environmental Protection Agency (EPA) in 1970, as well as for the first "Earth Day" on April 22, 1970.

Why We Connected with Environmentalism

The 60s ethos was wrapped around a fierce idealism embraced by maturing Boomers. Many Boomer young adults were concerned about equality for all people, and many of us believed the war in Vietnam was wrong. We also became painfully aware of the fragility of the earth, if not through Rachel Carson's book, then through our own understanding of pollution dangers in the world around us. Automobile recalls, oil spills, oceans and rivers polluted with toxins, and nuclear power plant meltdowns were just some of the events of the time that raised our environmental consciousness.

Gaylord Nelson, a Wisconsin Senator, was inspired by the student anti-war movement to create "Earth Day," a national day in support of environmental protection. Appalled by a 1969 California oil spill, Nelson, a Democrat, crossed the aisle to convince Pete McCloskey, a Republican Congressman, to co-chair a "national teach-in" on the environment. In order to encourage college students to participate, April 22 was selected because it fell between spring break and final exam week.

Earth Day was an opportunity for us to express our idealism in a broad, non-partisan way. Everyone could rally around saving the Earth. On April 22, 1970, some twenty million Americans took part in Earth Day demonstrations coast-to-coast. Maybe you were one of them. Earth Day has continued and expanded globally since then, becoming the largest secular observance in the world.

In the 70s, Boomers began to see green brands emerge as a direct result of an increased concern for the health and welfare of the environment. The earliest green brands boasted "back to nature" and revolved around organic foods and pure, natural ingredients. Most of these early brands were not widely available, but they were the harbingers, heralding the beginning of what would become a green brand boom from the 80s through the 90s and beyond. Protection of the environment, coupled with the adverse effects of climate change, remains a primary concern of the Boomer generation.

The following trademarks and registered trademarks are the property of their respective holders: Ad Age, Ad Council, American Dental Association, America's Healthiest Grocery Store, Earth Day Network, Keep America Beautiful, Tom's of Maine, Whole Foods Market

Sources

https://en.wikipedia.org/wiki/Environmentalism

https://en.wikipedia.org/wiki/Environmental_movement_in_the_United_St ates

http://environmentalhistory.org/20th-century/sixties-1960-1969/

https://www.fastcompany.com/1568686/a-history-of-green-brands-1960s-and-1970s-doing-the-groundwork

http://www.rachelcarson.org/SilentSpring.aspx

https://www.nytimes.com/2015/11/27/automobiles/50-years-ago-unsafe-at-any-speed-shook-the-auto-world.html

https://www.earthday.org/about/the-history-of-earth-day/

https://www.nytimes.com/2013/07/17/business/media/decades-after-a-memorable-campaign-keep-america-beautiful-returns.html

https://www.kab.org/

http://www.fundinguniverse.com/company-histories/tom-s-of-maine-inc-history/

https://www.tomsofmaine.com/

https://www.wholefoodsmarket.com/company-info/whole-foods-market-history#wholefoodsmarket

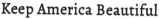

Keep America Beautiful

Keep America Beautiful, founded in 1953, is both a nonprofit organization and a national anti-pollution initiative. As a brand, it is probably best known for an advertising campaign that launched on Earth Day in 1971. Using the theme, "People Start Pollution. People Can Stop It," ads featured a character meant to represent an American Indian who shed a tear when he saw people littering. The public service campaign, which came to be known as the "crying Indian," ran until 1983 and was named by the trade publication *Ad Age* as one of the top 100 advertising campaigns of the 20th Century. Keep America Beautiful has continued to initiate campaigns designed to end littering, improve recycling, and beautify communities. However, some controversy has surrounded the organization over the years, because it was originally founded by cigarette and beverage manufacturers who have themselves been accused of irresponsible environmental practices. Still, most of us will never forget the "crying Indian," who, it turns out, was an actor of Italian origin just portraying one!

Photo credit: Printed material, Ad Council

Tom's of Maine

Tom's of Maine, one of the earliest green brands, was started in 1970 by Tom Chappell, a former insurance benefits counselor, and his wife Kate, an artist and poet. In 1968, they relocated to Kennebunk, Maine from Philadelphia, Pennsylvania, seeking out a simpler life and a healthier, more natural environment. Tom and Kate had a hard time finding natural products, so in 1970, they started Tom's Natural Soaps. The company made Clearlake, the first phosphate-free liquid laundry detergent in the U.S. The label was hand-drawn by Kate, and the product was packaged in containers that could be returned for refilling. A line of natural soaps, rinses, and shampoos followed in 1972, and an all-natural toothpaste was introduced in 1975. The fluoride version became the first natural brand to be approved by the American Dental Association. In the 1980s, Tom's of Maine emphasized philanthropy, donating a portion of its profits to environmental and human needs causes. The brand became part of the Colgate-Palmolive Company in 2006.

Photo credit: Tom's of Maine website

Whole Foods Market

Whole Foods is one of the first national natural foods store brands to leverage the back-to-nature movement of the 70s. In 1978, John Mackey and Renee Lawson (Hardy), both in their twenties, borrowed $45,000 and opened SaferWay, a small natural foods store in Austin, Texas. Two years later, they joined with Craig Weller and Mark Skiles, who ran the Clarksville Natural Grocery, to create a natural foods supermarket. The four partners opened the original Whole Foods Market in September 1980. The store was virtually wiped out by a flood the following year, but the business recovered thanks to the efforts of customers and neighbors. Expansion into Houston and Dallas and then to California followed in the 80s. Whole Foods Market then experienced rapid growth in the 90s when it acquired numerous other natural foods chains across the country. Still headquartered in Austin, today Whole Foods Market calls itself "America's Healthiest Grocery Store" and has over 400 stores in the United States, Canada and the United Kingdom. In 2017, Whole Foods Market was acquired by Amazon.

Photo credit: Whole Foods Market website

Ten Boomer Era Brands with Lasting Legacies

This bonus chapter highlights ten brands that were born during our growing up years. While these brands didn't target Boomer children specifically, they're in this book because they were created or popularized during the Boomer era and their legacies are lasting. You'll not only recognize these brands from your childhood, they very likely have influenced your adult life.

The following trademarks and registered trademarks are the property of their respective holders: Alka-Seltzer, Alka-Seltzer Plus, Amana, American Express, BankAmericard, Bank of America, Carte Blanche, Computer City, Dayton-Hudson, Diner's Club, Famous Brand Electronics, Fearless Flyer, Gatorade, Guess, Holiday Inn, Hush Puppies, Incredible Universe, Inter-Continental Hotels, Master Card, McDuff, Mickey Mouse, PepsiCo, Pronto Markets, Quaker Oats, Radarange, Radio Shack, Raytheon, Realistic, Salvatore Ferragamo, Sharp, Speedy Alka-Seltzer, Stokely-Van Camp, Super Bowl,

Tandy, Tappan, Target, Timex, Timex Ironman, Trader Joe's, Video Concepts, Visa, Walmart, Waterbury Clock

Sources

https://en.wikipedia.org/wiki/Alka-Seltzer

http://adage.com/article/adage-encyclopedia/alka-seltzer/98309/

https://www.alkaseltzer.com/

https://www.creditcards.com/credit-card-news/history-of-credit-cards.php

https://en.wikipedia.org/wiki/Credit_card

https://www.dinersclubus.com/home/about/dinersclub/story

https://en.wikipedia.org/wiki/Gatorade

http://www.research.ufl.edu/publications/explore/v08n1/gatorade.html

http://fortune.com/2015/10/01/gatorade-turns-50/

https://en.wikipedia.org/wiki/Holiday_Inn

http://business.time.com/2012/08/01/how-holiday-inn-changed-the-way-we-travel/

https://www.ihgplc.com/about-us/our-history

https://en.wikipedia.org/wiki/Hush_Puppies

http://selectedbrands.com/read-more-about-hush-puppies

https://www.hushpuppies.com/US/en/about-us/

https://en.wikipedia.org/wiki/RadioShack

https://en.wikipedia.org/wiki/Tandy_Corporation

https://www.twice.com/retailing/radioshack-brief-history-time-56040

https://dealbook.nytimes.com/2014/09/16/for-radioshack-a-history-of-misses/

https://www.usatoday.com/story/money/2018/07/26/radioshack-plans-open-100-express-locations/843010002/

https://en.wikipedia.org/wiki/History_of_Target_Corporation

https://corporate.target.com/about/history/Target-through-the-years

http://time.com/3831361/first-target-store/

https://money.cnn.com/2018/08/22/news/companies/target-walmart-amazon-costco/index.html

https://en.wikipedia.org/wiki/Timex_Group_USA

https://theidleman.com/manual/arrivals/brands/history-timex-watches/

https://www.timex.com/the-timex-story/

https://en.wikipedia.org/wiki/Trader_Joe%27s

https://www.traderjoes.com/our-story

https://www.thedailymeal.com/eat/10-things-you-didn-t-know-about-trader-joe-s

https://en.wikipedia.org/wiki/Microwave_oven

https://www.popularmechanics.com/technology/gadgets/a341/2078467/

Alka-Seltzer

Alka-Seltzer, made up of aspirin, sodium bicarbonate and citric acid, came to market in 1931, not during the Boomer era. However, Alka-Seltzer's dizzying popularity hit its high point in the 60s. It really began with "Speedy Alka-Seltzer," a fictional spokesperson created in the 50s. Speedy was a diminutive, smiling character with one Alka-Seltzer tablet for a body and another for a hat. While he first appeared in magazine ads in 1952, the animated Speedy on television endeared the little guy to adults and kids alike. Speedy became such a renowned advertising figure that he was reproduced in ads, on billboards and made into promotional giveaways and toys. With his effervescing magic wand, Speedy cheerily promised, "Relief is just a swallow away." Advertising in the 60s catapulted Alka-Seltzer to enduring fame. Animated ads with the theme and jingle, "No matter what shape your stomach's in," were so well-received that a rock group, the T-Bones, recorded a version of the song that became a 1966 hit. Other verbal gems from Alka-Seltzer ads included, "Mama mia, that's a spicy meatball," "I can't believe I ate the whole thing," and "Try it, you'll like it." In the 70s, Alka-Seltzer maintained its momentum with the catchy jingle,

"Plop plop, fizz fizz, oh what a relief it is." The product's memorable slogans quickly entered the lexicon of Boomer kids, making "Alka-Seltzer" both a household word and remedy. Today's Alka-Seltzer comes in "ReliefChews" and "Gummies" in addition to the original formulation. Alka-Seltzer also entered a new product category with "Alka-Seltzer Plus," a cold medicine.

Photo credit: M3MO on VisualHunt.com. Licensed under the Creative Commons Attribution 2.0 Generic license.

Credit Card

The ubiquitous, and some would say insidious, modern-day credit card was born in 1950. While credit vehicles such as airline, department store and oil company credit cards existed before then, Diner's Club introduced the first "general purpose" charge card in 1950. In its initial year, the cardboard card was limited to twenty-eight restaurants and two hotels, so it was really intended for business travel and entertainment. Carte Blanche and American Express, the first to take advantage of a worldwide network, followed soon after with credit cards of their own. American Express is also credited with issuing the first plastic credit card; all credit cards transitioned to plastic in the 60s. Technically, these early cards were charge cards, not credit cards, because monthly bills had to be paid in full. Banks turned charge cards into "credit" cards when they offered revolving credit so consumers could pay off their bills over time. The BankAmericard, introduced by Bank of America in 1958 only in California, was the first true credit card, and in 1966, it became a national credit card program. BankAmericard was renamed "Visa" ten years later. Meanwhile, a group of California banks decided to compete with BankAmericard, so

MasterCard was launched. Both systems featured interbank cooperation, which made them grow exponentially. Initially, banks could offer only one or the other, but today, banks and other financial institutions may offer both the Visa and MasterCard brands. Visa and MasterCard have kept up with the times by expanding into debit cards, gift cards, and rewards cards.

Photo credit: Frankieleon on VisualHunt.com. Licensed under the Creative Commons Attribution 2.0 Generic license.

Gatorade

Gatorade, the magic elixir that is credited with starting the sports drink category, was conceived in 1965 at the University of Florida, home to the Florida "Gators." Assistant football coach Dwayne Douglas asked a university researcher, Dr. Robert Cade, why players lost so much weight during practices and games but didn't need to urinate. Cade realized the cause was sweating, leading to a research project to determine why athletes also lost energy, strength and endurance when they sweated. Cade and his team of researchers believed that electrolytes, in particular sodium and potassium, were literally sweated out, upsetting the body's delicate chemical balance. With the blessing of head coach Ray Graves, the scientists tested their hypothesis on the football players and found that, after playing, the athletes' electrolytes were indeed out of balance and their blood sugar was low. Cade came up with a solution, literally – water supplemented with salt and sugar. It didn't taste very good until Cade's wife suggested adding lemon juice. That's when "Gatorade" was born. The first use of the concoction took place in an inter-squad game and the results looked promising. The next day, as the temperature soared to 102 degrees, the Gators defeated LSU; Gatorade was credited with replenishing the athletes' bodies. The football Gators ended the 1966 season with an 8-2 record and won their first ever Orange Bowl in 1967. The rights to Gatorade were sold by the University to Stokely-Van Camp, who marketed the product nationally for thirteen years, until the company was purchased by Quaker Oats. As part of the Quaker Oats Company, Gatorade secured 80 percent of the sports beverage market. The Gatorade brand is now a part of PepsiCo. It is aggressively marketed, enjoys the endorsement of major sports teams, personalities, and leagues, and continues to dominate its category.

Photo credit: Jeepers Media on VisualHunt.com. Licensed under the Creative Commons Attribution 2.0 Generic license.

Holiday Inn

On a road trip with his family in 1952, businessman Kemmons Wilson wondered why there couldn't be dependable, consistent hotels around the country that families could rely on during their vacations. Wilson opened a hotel in Memphis, Tennessee that featured clean rooms, comfortable beds, televisions, telephones, a swimming pool, free ice, and a restaurant – all conveniences not commonly available at the time. Affordability was just as important; unlike other hotels, Wilson didn't charge extra for children. He named the hotel "Holiday Inn," recalling a decade-old Bing Crosby movie of the same name. Wilson's real genius, though, was adopting the restaurant franchising model and applying it to his hotel. In 1954, Holiday Inn became the first hotel brand to franchise, using Wilson's original hotel as the model for others. Just two years later, the large, welcoming Holiday Inn road sign adorned U.S. highways and the chain became the first hotel brand to reach 300,000 rooms. Holiday Inn continued to innovate, introducing the first computerized hotel reservation system in 1965. By 1972, Holiday Inn was a major international chain, opening a new hotel every three days. Already the largest hotel chain in the world in 2007, Holiday

Inn launched a massive rebranding effort that included updating its logo, selling off inferior properties and refurbishing its remaining hotels. Today, the Holiday Inn brand, along with Holiday Inn Express, continues to thrive as part of InterContinental Hotels Group (IHG).

Photo credit: David Guo's Master on VisualHunt.com. Licensed under the Creative Commons Attribution 2.0 Generic license.

Hush Puppies

There's an excellent chance your parents wore Hush Puppies in the 50s or 60s. Maybe you did too. America's first truly casual shoes, Hush Puppies were developed by Wolverine in 1958. They were made of pigskin or brushed suede over a crepe rubber sole. The brand was named by a Wolverine sales manager who was enjoying a country dinner with a farmer. He learned that the deep-fried corn fritters he was eating were called "hush puppies" because they were thrown to barking farm dogs to quiet them. Tired feet were also known as "barking dogs" at the time, so the sales manager thought the company's new comfortable, quiet shoes were deserving of the same name. A photograph of a basset hound was chosen as the brand's logo when "Hush Puppies" was trademarked in 1958. The sad-eyed dog has remained the brand mark ever since. By 1963, Hush Puppies were very popular, gracing the feet of ten percent of the adult population of the United States. They were all the rage among celebrities around the world, including the notorious "Rat Pack," former president Eisenhower, and Prince Phillip of England. Hush Puppies started to fall out of favor in 1994, but the following year, they were revived by fashion designers who embraced 50s-era clothing styles. As a result, Hush Puppies began selling again and were awarded the "best accessory" prize at the 1996 Council of Fashion Designers awards dinner. Today the resilient Hush Puppies brand offers a variety of shoe styles for women, men and children.

Photo credit: France1978 on VisualHunt.com. Licensed under the Creative Commons Attribution ShareAlike 2.0 Generic license.

Microwave Oven

"Microwave" is a generic brand name that revolutionized mealtime and contributed to the meteoric rise of quick-cooking convenience foods in America. The heating quality of radio waves was said to have been discovered accidentally by Percy Spencer, an engineer who was working on radar for the Raytheon Company, when he noticed that it melted a chocolate bar he had in his pocket. Spencer decided to experiment by putting a kernel of corn near the radar; he ended up essentially creating the first microwave popcorn. A commercially available microwave, the 750-pound "Radarange," was introduced by Raytheon in 1947. The Tappan Stove Company licensed the technology from Raytheon and attempted to introduce a consumer version without much success. It wasn't until the mid-60s, when Sharp of Japan introduced the first turntable microwave oven to cook food evenly, that the microwave really caught on. In 1967, Raytheon's Amana brand brought a countertop Radarange to the home market, and then a proliferation of other brands followed. The microwave oven became so universally accepted that the individual brand names were almost secondary in importance. Originally thought to be dangerous, microwave ovens today are considered safe. They are available as built-in, under counter and standalone models and are standard appliances in most American homes.

Photo credit: Joshua Davis Photography on VisualHunt.com. Licensed under the Creative Commons Attribution ShareAlike 2.0 Generic license.

Radio Shack

Radio Shack, the forerunner of "big box" electronics stores such as Best Buy, was started as a ham radio supply store in 1921 in Boston by two brothers, Theodore and Milton Deutschmann. It wasn't until 1954, however, that the store became more widely known for "Realistic," Radio Shack's own brand of radio, stereo and electronics products. Radio Shack's national awareness also benefited from its mail order catalog operation, which started in the 1930s. After it was acquired in 1962 by Tandy Corporation, Radio Shack dramatically expanded in the 70s through a network of small, local stores. The locations were largely determined from customers in the mail order database. (That's the reason you were always asked to provide your address at a Radio Shack store, even if you were only buying a battery. You were sure to be sent a catalog.) Once the ham radio business declined, Radio Shack attempted to resurrect its brand by first entering the computer market and then the mobile phone market. The 1977 "TRS-80" (Tandy Radio Shack), an early computer for consumers, looked promising, but it was eventually overshadowed by the entry of Apple and IBM into the personal computer space. Radio Shack may have fallen prey to a bad brand moniker out of step with the times; the company seemed to admit that when it opened specialty stores with different names, such as Computer City, Famous Brand Electronics, McDuff, Video Concepts, and Incredible Universe. Despite efforts to revive "America's technology store," including a 2014 Super Bowl ad, the Radio Shack brand went bankrupt in 2015 and again in 2017. Somehow, the brand won't die, though: Its new owner, General Wireless Operations, announced "Radio Shack Express" locations would be opened inside Hobby Town stores beginning in 2018.

Photo credit: Jeepers Media on VisualHunt.com. Licensed under the Creative Commons Attribution 2.0 Generic license.

Target

Target began in 1962 as an upscale discount retailer, but its roots go back to 1902. That's when George D. Dayton started the Dayton Dry Goods Company in Minneapolis, Minnesota which, by 1911, became known as Dayton's Department Store. In the mid-50s, Dayton's began expanding to suburban Minneapolis, but the company came up with a novel concept in 1962: A new kind of discount store targeting value-oriented shoppers who were interested in quality. According to Target Corporation (the new name of the Dayton-Hudson Corporation as of 2000), the name Target was chosen because, "As a marksman's goal is to hit the center bulls-eye, the new store would do much the same in terms of retail goods, services, commitment to the community, price, value and overall experience." The concept was a direct hit; four years after its first opening in Minnesota, Target expanded into the Denver metropolitan area. In 1968, Target opened stores in the St. Louis, Dallas and Houston metro areas. By 1979, Target achieved $1 billion in annual sales. The lynchpin of the chain's success was "cheap chic," embodied in Target's ability to attract renowned designers who created fashions exclusively for the store. These lines, aimed at a more affluent customer, are part of the Target experience, which has humorously been branded "Tar-jay" in a jocular jab at the snootiness of its appeal. Target hasn't remained unscathed by the challenges of retail – the chain had to close down its unsuccessful Canadian operation, and growth has slowed in recent years. Still, it is redesigning stores, expanding store brands, lowering prices, and shoring up online operations, putting Target in a strong position to compete with its larger rival, Walmart, even as other traditional retailers flounder.

Photo credit: Jeepers Media on VisualHunt.com. Licensed under the Creative Commons Attribution 2.0 Generic license.

Timex

The brand name "Timex" was created in 1950 by the United States Time Corporation. The forerunner of the company, the Waterbury Clock Company, was the first to create a mass-produced affordable timepiece in 1854. After the Great Depression depressed the company's sales, a mouse came to the rescue. Under its Ingersoll brand name, Waterbury produced Mickey Mouse wristwatches in the 1930s, accounting for $1 million in sales and the company's revival. Waterbury then manufactured precision timers for the country in World War II, after which it was renamed United States Time Corporation. Prior to Timex, Swiss watch movements were standard in watches, but they were expensive because of their jeweled movements. The Timex watch incorporated the first high quality mass-produced watch movement, using a new material for bearings. As a result, Timex watches gained a reputation for reliability, durability, superior design and affordability. In the late 50s, Timex became renowned for a series of television ads featuring John Cameron Swayze, who did everything he could to destroy a Timex watch on live television. When he failed, as he always did, he proclaimed solemnly, "Timex. Takes a licking and keeps on ticking." That campaign helped propel Timex into consumer brand consciousness so that by the end of the decade, every third watch sold in the U.S. was a Timex. Timex continued to innovate, issuing the first sports watch (Timex Ironman) in 1984; it became the best-selling sports watch in the world for a decade. In 1969, the United States Time Corporation was renamed Timex Corporation. Today, the Timex Group markets Timex and Guess watches, as well as luxury watch brands such as Salvatore Ferragamo Timepieces and Valentino Timeless.

Photo credit: Photo on VisualHunt.com. Licensed under the Creative Commons Attribution 2.0 Generic license.

Trader Joe's

The "Joe" who started Trader Joe's, Joe Coulombe, first ran a small chain of convenience stores called Pronto Markets in the late 50s. In 1967, Joe decided to open a specialty grocery store in Pasadena, California, naming it "Trader Joe's." A chain of Polynesian-style restaurants called "Trader Vic's" was popular at the time. Joe picked up on the South Seas theme, adorning his store with a nautical theme, a captain's bell, and Hawaiian shirts for employees. Joe's concept was to source unique foods and eventually sell most of them under the Trader Joe's brand name at competitive prices. All of these elements can be found in today's Trader Joe's stores – relatively small specialty grocery outlets around the U.S., over 470 of them including the original Pasadena store. More than eighty percent of the inventory in the stores is sold under the Trader Joe's brand. The California-based company watches food trends closely and often adds one-of-a-kind products that seem to have a special appeal to Boomers. A typically quirky Trader Joe's feature is the "Fearless Flyer," a periodic publication that highlights trending items and replaces the traditional grocery store sales flyer. Trader

Joe's never offers items "on sale" but instead features affordability as part of its brand promise. Trader Joe's consistently ranks as one of the country's top grocery chains in customer satisfaction, as well as maintaining one of the highest ratios of sales per square foot in the industry. Trader Joe's has become known for innovation, quality products at reasonable prices, a folksy, friendly atmosphere, accommodating customer service, and excellent treatment of employees.

Photo credit: Tony Webster on VisualHunt.com. Licensed under the Creative Commons Attribution 2.0 Generic license.

Birth of the Modern Brand

Thanks for joining me on this nostalgic journey through Boomer Brandland. I hope you had fun reliving your childhood and remembering some of the iconic brands of the 50s and 60s. Perhaps you also gained an appreciation for the essential role brands play in our everyday lives.

The Boomer era was a period of time that represented the birth of the modern brand. During our childhood, brands became marketing superstars. Each brand was created for a specific audience and managed as a distinct commercial entity. Many of the brands born during our childhood remain vibrant brands today.

The Boomer era was unique from a branding perspective. It was the first time brands could be marketed in a coordinated, multimedia fashion, using newspapers, magazines, direct mail, radio, outdoor, and television in combination. It was the first time brands could advertise on television, sponsor television shows, and exert their influence on a broad audience.

So let's pay homage to the early days of television. Boomers were the first generation to grow up watching television. TV entertained and educated us in a way no medium had ever done before, even if we unwittingly became brand ambassadors and promotional conduits to our parents.

The Boomer era was the time you and I started a lengthy love affair with brands. Those brands we were introduced to as kids are the "Boomer Brands" we still remember today. They are brands we will never forget.

The Boomer Era, Year by Year

The "Baby Boomer" generation refers to those of us who were born between 1946 and 1964, a period of eighteen years during which the U.S. population saw a "baby boom," or an annual spike in births. The goal of *Boomer Brands* was to discuss popular brands during that time period, but not to cover specific years. Still, you might be curious to know what was happening in the brand world the year you were born. This Appendix lists some of those "Boomer Brands," as well as other fun facts, for each of the eighteen Boomer era years.

Sources

https://www.bbhq.com/bomrstat.htm

https://www.history.com/topics/baby-boomers

http://www.thepeoplehistory.com/1946.html
(and subsequent years)

https://en.wikipedia.org/wiki/Category:American_companies_established_i
n_1946
(and subsequent years)

1946

Number of American Boomers born this year:
3.411 million
(20 percent more than in 1945)

Notable American companies/brands started this year:
Aloha Airlines
Best Western Hotels
Estée Lauder Companies
Fender Musical Instruments Corporation
Hy-Tone Records
Iams
Tektronix
Tonka
Tupperware Brands
UNIVAC

Brand and Cultural News of the Year:
Tupperware food containers are introduced in the United States, but Tupperware home parties do not begin until 1948.

The bikini is introduced in Paris amidst controversy. Widely accepted throughout Europe in the 50s, the bikini is still banned in some places and is not popular in the United States until the 60s.

The first Cannes Film Festival takes place.

1947

Number of American Boomers born this year:
3.817 million

Notable American companies/brands started this year:
Capital Cities (later purchased ABC)
Igloo Coolers
Los Angeles Airways
Magazine Management
(publisher of film, men's, and romance magazines)

Brand and Cultural News of the Year:
The microwave oven is invented.

Bazooka bubble gum is introduced by the Topps Company.

Italian company Ferrari begins making sports cars.

The first Polaroid Land Camera is demonstrated.

The Diary of Anne Frank is published.

1948

Number of American Boomers born this year:
3.637 million

Notable American companies/brands started this year:
Capital Airlines
Dick's Sporting Goods
Korvette department stores
Piedmont Airlines
Toys "R" Us
True Value stores
Velcro
Wham-O

Brand and Cultural News of the Year:
Nestle Quik is introduced.

German care company Porsche is founded.

The first Polaroid Land Camera is sold in Boston, Mass.

The Long Playing (LP) record is invented.

The transistor radio is invented.

One million households around the world own a television.

1949

Number of American Boomers born this year:
3.649 million

Notable American companies/brands started this year:
Automatic Data Processing (ADP)
Norm Thompson Outfitters
Pacific Southwest Airlines
Silly Putty
Southern Airways
Strand Bookstore (New York)

Brand and Cultural News of the Year:
The first Volkswagen Beetle is sold in the U.S.

The first Porsche car is shown at an auto show.

The first 45 RPM record is introduced.

"Bozo the Clown" first appears on television.

"Hopalong Cassidy" is the first Western to appear on television.

The National Basketball Association (NBA) is founded.

1950

Number of American Boomers born this year:
3.632 million

Notable American companies/brands started this year:
Aurora Plastics Corporation
Clearasil
David's Bridal
Desilu Productions (producer of "I Love Lucy")
Dunkin' Donuts
Jack in the Box restaurants
Timex watches
Walter Lantz Productions (animation studio)

Brand and Cultural News of the Year:

Diner's Club issues the first credit card.

The Disney film "Cinderella" debuts.

James Dean starts his career by appearing in a Pepsi commercial.

The first television remote control is introduced.

Eight million homes in the U.S. own a television.

1951

Number of American Boomers born this year:
3.823 million

Notable American companies/brands started this year:
Iron Mountain
Scientific Atlanta
Texas Instruments
Universal Television
Wang Laboratories

Brand and Cultural News of the Year:

The term "Rock 'n' Roll" is used for the first time.

"Watch Mr. Wizard" first appears on television.

"I Love Lucy" debuts on the CBS television network.

The Disney Movie "Alice in Wonderland" premieres.

"Dennis the Menace" first appears in newspapers.

The birth control pill is developed.

1952

Number of American Boomers born this year:
3.913 million

Notable American companies/brands started this year:
Allegheny Airlines
Aqua Lung America
Chevrolet Corvette
Chicken Delight
Church's Chicken
Holiday Inn
Kellogg's "Sugar Frosted Flakes"
Mr. Potato Head
Mrs. T's Pierogies
Sheetz
The Timberland Company
Walt Disney Imagineering

Brand and Cultural News of the Year:
   Austrian candy PEZ comes to the U.S.

   Ban, the first roll-on deodorant, is introduced.

   Kentucky Fried Chicken is franchised.

   MAD magazine is published.

1953

Number of American Boomers born this year:
3.965 million

Notable American companies/brands started this year:
Burger King
Chevrolet Corvette
Denny's
Kaiser Jeep
Keep America Beautiful
Panavision
STP motor oil
Walt Disney Studios Motion Pictures

Brand and Cultural News of the Year:
The Chevrolet Corvette goes on sale.

Cheez Whiz is introduced by Kraft.

The WIFFLE ball is introduced.

The Disney film "Peter Pan" debuts.

The first color television goes on sale in the U.S.

The first James Bond novel (*Casino Royale* by Ian Fleming) is published.

1954

Number of American Boomers born this year:
4.078 million

Notable American companies/brands started this year:
American Motors Corporation
Broaster Company
Burger Chef
Mego Corporation (toys)
Realistic (Radio Shack brand)
Taco Bell
Varsity Bus (school buses)

Brand and Cultural News of the Year:
Swanson introduces TV dinners.

Howard Johnson Motor Lodges first appear.

The Disney film "20,000 Leagues Under the Sea" is released.

"Rock Around the Clock" is released by Bill Haley and
The Comets.

A rock 'n' roll performer named Elvis Presley starts
his career.

1955

Number of American Boomers born this year:
4.097 million

Notable American companies/brands started this year:
Atco Records
Cadet Records
Liberty Records
MGM Television
Volkswagen Group of America
Wellcraft (powerboats)

Brand and Cultural News of the Year:
Crest toothpaste is marketed for the first time.

The McDonald's franchise system is launched by Ray Kroc.

"The Mickey Mouse Club" premieres on the ABC television network.

"Gunsmoke" appears on television for the first time.

The Broadway show "Peter Pan" is broadcast live on television.

Disneyland opens.

1956

Number of American Boomers born this year:
4.218 million

Notable American companies/brands started this year:
Jersey Mike's Subs
Mr. Donut
Mr. Softee
Sbarro

Brand and Cultural News of the Year:

The black-and-white portable television is introduced.

The film "The Ten Commandments" debuts.

"As the World Turns," the first half-hour daytime serial, appears on the CBS television network.

Elvis Presley releases his first hit ("Heartbreak Hotel") and appears on The Ed Sullivan Show.

Actress Grace Kelly marries Prince Rainier of Monaco.

1957

Number of American Boomers born this year:
4.3 million

Notable American companies/brands started this year:
Dick Clark Productions
DuPont Central Research
Fairchild Semiconductor
Frisbee
Hanna-Barbera
Sir Pizza
Stax Records
Tang

Brand and Cultural News of the Year:
The Frisbee is introduced by Wham-O.

Tang is invented.

American Bandstand debuts on national television on the ABC television network.

Cars made by the Japanese automaker, Toyota, are introduced into the U.S.

Elvis Presley purchases Graceland in Memphis, Tennessee.

1958

Number of American Boomers born this year:
4.255 million

Notable American companies/brands started this year:
"Alpha-Bits" by Post Cereals
Beginner Books (publisher of Dr. Seuss)
Cost Plus World Market
Edsel
Hula Hoop
Hush Puppies
The Jim Henson Company (creator of "The Muppets")
Pizza Hut
Tandem Productions (producer of "All in the Family")
United Artists Television
Warner Music Group

Brand and Cultural News of the Year:
The Hula Hoop is introduced by Wham-O.

BankAmericard, the first bank credit card, is issued.

Ford introduces the ill-fated Edsel.

"Huckleberry Hound" first appears on television.

The peace symbol is created.

1959

Number of American Boomers born this year:
4.245 million

Notable American companies/brands started this year:
Barbie doll
Bluesville Records
Motown
National Convenience Stores (Stop-N-Go Foods)
Ron Jon Surf Shop
Round Table Pizza
Sonic
Sport Chalet

Brand and Cultural News of the Year:
The Barbie doll is introduced by Mattel.

The film "Ben Hur" debuts.

"Bonanza" premieres on the NBC television network as the first weekly series to be broadcast completely in color.

"The Twilight Zone" hosted by Rod Serling premieres on the CBS television network.

Buddy Holly, Richie Valens, and The Big Bopper are killed in a plane crash.

1960

Number of American Boomers born this year:
4.258 million

Notable American companies/brands started this year:
Etch A Sketch
Famous Footwear
Hardee's
Loews Hotels
Record Bar
Redken
SeaWorld Parks & Entertainment
Sony Corporation of America
Tower Records
Vitamin World

Brand and Cultural News of the Year:
"The Twist" by Chubby Checker becomes a national dance sensation.

The Alfred Hitchcock film, "Psycho," premieres.

Aluminum cans are introduced to consumers.

There are over 100 million television sets worldwide.

John F. Kennedy is elected President of the United States.

1961

Number of American Boomers born this year:
4.268 million

Notable American companies/brands started this year:
Claire's
Giorgio Beverly Hills
Humana
K2 Sports
"Life" cereal by the Quaker Oats Company
Pampers
Raggedy Ann and Andy dolls
Red Barn restaurants

Brand and Cultural News of the Year:
  Pampers disposable diapers are introduced.

  The movie, "West Side Story," premieres.

  "The Dick Van Dyke Show" airs on the CBS television network.

  "The Avengers" premieres on British television.

  Squibb introduces the first electric toothbrush.

1962

Number of American Boomers born this year:
4.167 million

Notable American companies/brands started this year:
Ascena Retail Group (owner of Ann Taylor and Lane Bryant)
Cadence Industries (owner of Marvel Comics Group)
Kampgrounds of America (KOA)
Kmart
Little Caesar's
Motel 6
St. John (clothing)
Target
Univision
Walmart
Woolco stores

Brand and Cultural News of the Year:
 The first song by The Beatles ("Love Me Do") is released in the U.K.

 Spider-Man first appears in a Marvel comic book.

 The Silent Spring by Rachel Carson is published.

 Marilyn Monroe dies of a drug overdose.

1963

Number of American Boomers born this year:
4.098 million

Notable American companies/brands started this year:
Comcast
CVS Pharmacy
The Limited
MCI Communications
Pennzoil

Brand and Cultural News of the Year:
The "smiley face" is invented by an insurance company.

"Beatlemania" begins to spread across the world.

The lava lamp is introduced.

The touch tone phone is invented.

The tape cassette is invented.

The pop-top can is first used.

ZIP codes are instituted in the U.S.

President John F. Kennedy is assassinated.

1964

Number of American Boomers born this year:
4.027 million

Notable American companies/brands started this year:
Arby's
Bose Corporation
Ford Mustang
The Franklin Mint
Hasbro's G.I. Joe toys
Kellogg's Pop-Tarts

Brand and Cultural News of the Year:
   "Buffalo Wings" are invented in Buffalo, New York

Pop-Tarts are introduced by Kellogg's.

The first Mustang automobile comes on the market.

The Beatles' first album is released in the U.S., they hold the top five positions in the Billboard Top 40, and they first appear on The Ed Sullivan Show.

Unsafe at Any Speed by Ralph Nader is published.

The first VCR is introduced by Sony.

Boomer Brands Index

In order to make this index more useful, it is set up in a non-conventional way. Brand references are indexed alphabetically within each chapter rather than as part of a lengthy single list. In addition, "Boomer Brand Cameos" for each chapter are identified for easy reference.

Wagon Train, Watch Mr. Wizard, Winky Dink and You, The Woody Woodpecker Show, Yogi Bear

Boomer Brand Cameos:

Bozo the Clown

Huckleberry Hound

Mr. Wizard

Westerns

Bowled Over ....25 – 33

(Cereal brands)

Alpha-Bits, American Bandstand, Cap'n Crunch, Cheerios, Chex, Cocoa Krispies, Cocoa Puffs, Corn Flakes, Disney, Froot Loops, General Mills, Grape-Nuts, Kellogg's, Kellogg's Frosted Flakes, Kellogg's Rice Krispies, Kix, Life, Lone Ranger, Lucky Charms, Maypo, Mickey Mouse Club, Post Cereals, Post Toasties, Puffed Rice, Puffed Wheat, Quaker Oats, Ralston Purina, Rice Krinkles, Rocky and Bullwinkle, Sugar Pops, The Breakfast of Champions, Tony the Tiger, Trix, Wheaties

Boomer Brand Cameos:

Frosted Flakes

Cheerios

Alpha-Bits

Life

Soda Pop-ular ....35 – 41

(Soft drink brands)

7Up, A&W, Coca-Cola, Coke, Crush, Dr Pepper, Hawaiian Punch, Hi-C, Kool-Aid, Mott, NASA Orange Crush, Pepsi, Pepsi-Cola, Pepsi Generation, RC Cola, Tab, Tang, The Real Thing, Things Go Better with Coke, Uncola, Welch, Yoo-hoo

Boomer Brand Cameos:

The Cola Wars

Fruit Juice Frenzy

Tang

Snack Attack ....43 – 52

(Snack food brands)

Almond Joy, Batman, Bazooka, Betty Crocker, Cheetos, Chips Ahoy!, Cracker Jack, Ding Dongs, Doritos, Dubble Bubble, EZ Pop, Fleer, Fritos, Goldfish, Good Humor, Ho Hos, Jiffy Pop, Junior Mints, Lay's, Mars, M&M, Hershey, Howard Johnson, Hostess, Merriam-Webster, Oreo, PEZ, Planter's, Pringles, Sno Balls, Tic Tacs, Tops, Twinkies, Twizzlers, Wise, Wrigley's Doublemint, Wrigley's Juicy Fruit, Wrigley's Spearmint

Boomer Brand Cameos:
Bubble Gum
Good Humor
Oreo
Twinkies

Faster Foods ....53 – 60
(Convenience food brands)
B&M, Campbell's, Captain Midnight, Charlie the Tuna, Cheez Whiz, Chiquita, Fluff, General Foods, Heinz, Jell-O, Jif, Kellogg's, Kraft, Lassie, M'm M'm Good!, Mott, Nestle, Nestle Quik, Ovaltine, Oscar Mayer, Pop-Tarts, Skippy, Smucker's, Smucker's Goober, SpaghettiOs, Starkist, Swanson, Wienermobile, Welch, Wonder Bread

Boomer Brand Cameos:
Cheese Whiz
Jell-O
Ovaltine

Playtime...61 – 69
(Toy and game brands)
Action Comics, Aurora, Barbie, Batman, Candyland, Careers, Chatty Cathy, Coca-Cola, Classics Illustrated, Concentration, DC Comics, Disney, Etch A Sketch, FAST COMPANY, Fisher-Price, Flexible Flyer, Frisbee, Game of Life, GI Joe, Hasbro, Hot Wheels, Hula Hoop, LEGO, LEGOLAND, Lincoln Logs, Lionel, Lone Ranger, Macy's, MAD, Matchbox, Milton Bradley, Monopoly, Mouse Trap, Mr. Potato Head, Operation, Polaroid, Pop-o-Matic, Radio Flyer, Revell, Rifleman, Rin Tin Tin, Risk, Schwinn, Scrabble, Silly Putty, Slinky, Stratego, Superman, Tiddly Winks, Trouble, Twister, View-Master, Wham-O, WIFFLE Ball, Yahtzee

Boomer Brand Cameos:
Board Games
LEGO
MAD
WIFFLE Ball

(Disney brands)
ABC, Disney, Disneyland, Disney World, Donald Duck, Goofy, Imagineer, Mickey Mouse, Mickey Mouse Club, Minnie Mouse, Mouseketeer, Pluto, Walt Disney
Boomer Brand Cameos:
Mickey Mouse Ears
Disney Parks and Resorts
Disney Merchandising

(Health and beauty brands)
American Bandstand, Benson & Hedges, Brylcreem, Bucky Beaver, Buster Brown, Camel, Cheerios, Chesterfield, Clairol, Clearasil, Colgate, Coppertone, Crest, Disney, Dove, Enovid, Ice O Derm, Ipana, Keds, Kent, Kool, L&M, Levi's, Lucky Strike, Marlboro, Mary Janes, Mennen, Old Spice, Pall Mall, Palmolive, Parliament, Pepsodent, Planned Parenthood, Prell, Revlon's Fire & Ice, Salem, Secret, Tareyton, Thom McAn Virginia Slims, Winston
Boomer Brand Cameos:
Clearasil
Coppertone
The Pill
Virginia Slims

(Car brands)
AMC, Buick Roadmaster, Bullitt, Cadillac, Camaro, Charger, Chevron, Chevy, Chevrolet, Chrysler, Cobra, Corvette, Dodge, Firebird, Fleetwood, Ford, General Motors, GM, Goldfinger, GTO, Hudson, Indianapolis 500,

James Bond, Mustang, Nash, Oldsmobile, Oldsmobile 88, Plymouth, Pontiac, Rambler American, Sting Ray, Texaco, Thunderbird, Volkswagen, VW
Boomer Brand Cameos:
Corvette
Mustang
Texaco

(Howard Johnson brands)
28, Bumbershoot's, Chatt's, Deli Baker Ice Cream Maker, Ground Round, Happy Meal, HoJo, HoJoLand, Howard Johnson, Howard Johnson's, McDonald's, Paddywacks, Pickle Lily's, Red Coach Grill, Wyndham Hotels
Boomer Brand Cameo:
HoJo Brands

(Fast food brands)
Arby's, Burger Chef, Burger King, Chick-fil-A, Coca-Cola, Coke, Domino's, Dunkin' Donuts, Hardees, In-N-Out, Jack in the Box, Kentucky Fried Chicken, KFC, Little Caesar's, McDonald's, Multimixer, Pizza Hut, Sonic, Subway, Taco Bell, Wendy's, White Castle, White Tower
Boomer Brand Cameos:
Kentucky Fried Chicken
McDonald's
Pizza Hut

(Rock 'n' roll brands)
American Bandstand, Atlantic, The Beatles, The Beach Boys, The Byrds, Capitol, The Coasters, Columbia, Cream, Creedence Clearwater Revival, Decca, The Dave Clark Five, Dion and the Belmonts, The Doors, The Drifters, Elektra, Epic, The Everly Brothers, The Four Seasons, The Four Tops, Grateful Dead, Hullabaloo, The Jackson Five, Jan and Dean, Jefferson Airplane, Jimi Hendrix Experience, The Kinks, Gladys Knight and the Pips, Lovin' Spoonful, Martha and the Vandellas, Mercury, The Monkees, Motown, The Platters, The Rascals, RCA, Reprise, Smokey Robinson and the Miracles, The

Rolling Stones, Shindig, Soul Train, Stax, Sun, The Shirelles, Simon & Garfunkel, The Supremes, The Temptations, The Who

Boomer Brand Cameos:

American Bandstand

The Monkees

Motown

(Consciousness brands)

Black Panther Party, Black Panthers, CORE, Moral Majority, NAACP, NOW, Woodstock

Boomer Brand Cameos:

Black Panther Party

Eugene McCarthy

Woodstock

(Green brands)

Ad Age, Ad Council, American Dental Association, America's Healthiest Grocery Store, Earth Day Network, Keep America Beautiful, Tom's of Maine, Whole Foods Market

Boomer Brand Cameos:

Keep America Beautiful

Tom's of Maine

Whole Foods Market

Alka-Seltzer

Credit Card

Gatorade

Holiday Inn

Hush Puppies

Microwave Oven

Radio Shack

Target

Timex

Trader Joe's

About the Author

Barry Silverstein is a Boomer, freelance writer and retired direct marketing/brand marketing professional. He is the author of numerous non-fiction marketing and small business books, including *Branding 123* and *The Breakaway Brand*. He also writes a blog for Boomers called "Happily Rewired" (http://www.happilyrewired.com). Silverstein resides with his wife in the Asheville, North Carolina area. Visit his website at: http://www.barrysilverstein.com

About the Publisher

GuideWords Publishing publishes books at the intersection of Boomers and business. *Boomer Brands* is the company's second book. Its first book, *Let's Make Money, Honey: The Couple's Guide to Starting a Service Business,* is designed to help couples succeed in starting and running a small service business. To learn more about GuideWords Publishing, visit the website: http://www.guidewordspub.com

Did you enjoy reading this book?

Word of mouth is so important to a book's ability to reach the right audience. If you enjoyed reading *Boomer Brands*, I hope you will consider recommending it to family, friends, and any Boomers you know who may want to recall popular brands of their era and reminisce about their childhood.

Please also consider posting a positive review online at Amazon.com or another website where you may have purchased this book.

Thank you!

Barry Silverstein

http://www.boomerbrandsbook.com